JAPANESE

HOME COOKING

Learn How to Prepare Japanese
Traditional Food with Over 100
Recipes for Ramen, Sushi, and
Vegetarian Dishes

Adele Tyler

CONTENTS

INTRODUCTION _____9

CHAPTER 1: INTRODUCTION TO JAPANESE FOOD __11

1.1 History and Origin of Japanese Food _____11

1.2 History of Traditional Japanese Dishes_____12

1.3 Evolution of Japanese Food over Time _____14

1.4 Popularity of Japanese Dishes in the U.S.A _____15

CHAPTER 2: HOME COOKING VS. DINE- IN
EXPERIENCE _____17

2.1 Difference between Home Cooking Vs. Dine-in Experience 18

2.2 Health Benefits of Japanese Food _____21

2.3 Different Properties of Spices used in Japanese Food _____23

CHAPTER 3: JAPANESE BREAKFAST RECIPES _____29

3.1 Japanese Omelette _____30

3.2 Breakfast Ramen _____31

3.3 Japanese Style Pancakes _____33

3.4 Japanese Breakfast Rice Bowl _____35

3.5 Tamagoyaki_____36

3.6 Tonkatsu _____37

3.7 Japanese Egg Omelette Sandwich _____38

3.8 Japanese Rolled Omelette _____39

3.9 Hiroshima Okonomiyaki_____41

3.10 Japanese Hibachi Style Fried Rice _____43

3.11 Japanese Breakfast Skillet _____44

CHAPTER 4: JAPANESE LUNCH AND DINNER RECIPES _____46

4.1 Onigiri _____46

4.2 Natto _____47

4.3 Agedashi Tofu _____48

4.4 Nasu Dengaku _____49

4.5 Omurice _____52

4.6 Okonomiyaki _____54

4.7 Cheesy Ramen Carbonara _____55

4.8 Yakisoba_____57

4.9 Baked chicken Katsu _____59

4.10 Hayashi Ground Beef Curry _____60

4.11 Ramen Noodle Skillet with Steak _____62

4.12 Chicken Teriyaki_____63

4.13 Japanese Salmon Bowl _____64

4.14 Scattered Sushi Rice/Chirashi-zushi_____66

4.15 Broiled Shrimp and Vegetables/ Kushiyaki _____68

4.16 Chicken in a Pot/Mizutaki_____69

CHAPTER 5: JAPANESE SALAD RECIPES _____ 71

5.1 Japanese cucumber Salad (Sunomo) _____ 71

5.2 Japanese Watercess Salad _____ 72

5.3 Kani Salad _____ 73

5.4 Oshitashi _____ 74

5.5 Japanese Cabbage Salad _____ 75

5.6 Ramen Noodle Salad _____ 75

5.7 Pork Chimichurri Salad _____ 77

5.8 Spring Green Salad _____ 78

5.9 Japanese Corn Salad _____ 80

CHAPTER 6: JAPANESE SOUP RECIPES _____ 81

6.1 Miso soup _____ 81

6.2 Ochazuke _____ 82

6.3 Ozoni _____ 82

6.4 Japanese Clear Onions Soup _____ 83

6.5 Wonton Dumplings Soup _____ 84

6.6 Kimchi and Tofu Soup _____ 85

6.7 Shio Koji Mushroom Soup _____ 86

6.8 Yudofu _____ 87

6.9 Ojiya Rice Soup _____ 88

6.10 Oshiruko Sweet Red Bean Soup _____ 88

6.11 Bean Paste Soup _____ 89

6.12 Egg Drop Soup _____90

CHAPTER 7: JAPANESE SNACKS _____91

7.1 Japanese Summer Sandwiches _____91

7.2 Fresh Spring Rolls with Japanese Style Sauce _____91

7.3 Karaage Japanese Fried Chicken _____93

7.4 Tazukuri Candied Sardines _____94

7.5 Kuromame Sweetened Black Soybean _____96

7.6 Takoyaki Octopus Balls _____97

7.7 Yakitori Grilled Skewers _____98

7.8 Sweet Ginger Meatballs _____100

7.9 Satsuma Age Fried Fish Cake with Vegetables _____101

7.10 Sweet and Salty Nori Seaweed Popcorn _____103

CHAPTER 8: JAPANESE DESSERTS _____104

8.1 Kinako Dango _____104

8.2 Japanese Style Pumpkin Pudding _____105

8.3 Dorayaki _____106

8.4 Fluffy Japanese Cheesecake _____107

8.5 Matcha Ice cream _____108

8.6 Taiyaki _____109

8.7 Zenzai _____110

8.8 Okoshi _____111

8.9 Dango_____112

8.10 Kasutera _____112

8.11 Daifuku_____114

CHAPTER 9: RAMEN AND SUSHI RECIPES _____115

9.1 Shoyu Ramen_____115

9.2 Miso Ramen _____116

9.3 Simple Homemade Chicken Ramen _____117

9.4 Vegetarian Ramen _____117

9.5 Ramen Noodles _____118

9.6 Pork Ramen _____118

9.7 Instant Ramen_____119

9.8 Sushi _____119

9.9 Japanese Sushi Rolls _____121

CHAPTER 10: MOST POPULAR AND ALTERNATIVE JAPANESE RECIPES _____123

10.1 Sashimi _____123

10.2 Unadon_____123

10.3 Tempura_____125

10.4 Soba _____126

10.5 Udon _____126

10.6 Sukiyaki_____127

10.7 Oden _____129

10.8 Gohan - Steamed Rice _____130

10.9 Tonkatsu _____131

10.10 Wagashi _____132

10.11 Japanese Matcha Green Tea _____133

CHAPTER 11: JAPANESE VEGETARIAN RECIPES ___134

11.1 Kenchin Vegetable Soup _____134

11.2 Vegan Japanese Omelette _____135

11.3 Japanese Vegetable Pancake _____136

11.4 Vegetarian Japanese Curry _____136

11.5 Vegetable Tempura _____138

11.6 Japanese Edamame _____139

11.7 Japanese Eggplant Curry _____140

11.8 Mushroom and Tofu Potstickers _____141

11.9 Vegetable Teppanyaki _____142

11.10 Naturally Sweet Red Bean Daifuku _____143

11.11 Japanese Carrot Pickles _____144

11.12 Mango Mochi _____144

11.13 Japanese Green Avocado Salad _____146

11.14 Sweet Potatoes and Avocado Green Salad _____147

11.15 Japanese Baked Sweet Potato _____148

11.16 Japanese Fried Rice _____149

11.17 Kenchinjiru _____151

Introduction

We all love to have food conveniently. Everyone loves to order food or get to some restaurant to have their favourite dishes but eating out can be unhealthy to a greater extent. Towards the end of a busy day, eating out or ordering your food might feel like the most convenient and the most straightforward choice. In any case, comfort and restaurant prepared food can negatively affect your health and wellbeing. One of the simplest ways to improve your health is by preparing more home-cooked meals.

Our world comprises of various countries with numerous types of cuisines that are being eaten all around the globe. One such cuisine is called the Japanese cuisine that is, as the name clearly depicts, originated from the Asian country, Japan.

Japanese cooking mainly includes the territorial and conventional nourishments of Japan, which have been developed through hundreds of years of political, monetary, and social changes. The customary cooking of Japan depends on rice with miso soup and different dishes; there is an accentuation on seasonal ingredients.

In this book regarding Japanese home cooking, we will discuss in detail the history as well as the origin of Japanese food and its evolution over the passage of time. You will also get a section in the book where you will learn the reason behind the popularity of Japanese cuisine in the U.S.A. In this book, you will get the knowledge regarding the difference between home cooking and dine in experience while having Japanese food.

There are various different kinds of spices being used in Japanese cooking, out of which many have been discussed in detail in the chapters below. You will learn different recipes, including breakfast, lunch, dinner, dessert, salad, soups, snacks, sushi, alternative, and traditional as well as vegetarian recipes. All the recipes mentioned in this book are extremely easy to make all on your own at home. Now, let us not brag too much and finally start cooking Japanese at home.

Chapter 1: Introduction to Japanese Food

Japanese cooking has been around for more than 2,000 years with its strong links from both China and Korea. Although, it has just been a couple of hundreds of years since all the impacts have come to form what is now known as Japanese cuisine. Japanese cooking has overwhelmed the culinary scene. With its one-of-a-kind taste of flavours and fragile mix of sweet and savory, it is no big surprise Japanese meals are so well known. From sushi to ramen, Japanese and Japanese-motivated dishes can be found worldwide, including your own kitchen. You do not need to be a master chef to bring home the exquisite flavours of Japanese cuisine.

Japanese individuals call every supper "Gohan." For instance, breakfast is classified "asa-Gohan." A bowl of steamed rice is included for every single Japanese dinner and is very important for breakfast, lunch, or supper. Side dishes are called okazu and are presented with rice and soup. Rice is a staple of the Japanese eating routine. Rice cakes (mochi) are additionally usually very common. They range from sweet to exquisite and have various preparations from bubbled to barbecued.

1.1 History and Origin of Japanese Food

Japanese cuisine has been influenced by the food customs of other nations but has adopted and refined them to create its own unique cooking style and eating habits. The first foreign influence on Japan was China around 300 B.C. when the Japanese learned to cultivate rice. The use of chopsticks and the consumption of soy sauce and soybean curd (tofu) also came from China.

The Buddhist religion, one of the two major religions in Japan today, was another important influence on the Japanese diet. In the A.D. 700s, the rise of Buddhism led to a ban on eating meat. The popular dish sushi came about as a result of this ban. In the 1800s, cooking styles became simpler. A wide variety of vegetarian foods were served in small portions, using one of five standard cooking techniques.

Starting in the mid-1200s, trade with different nations started bringing Western-style impacts to Japan. The Dutch presented corn, potatoes, and yams. The Portuguese presented tempura. After a boycott of more than 1,000 years, hamburger got back to Japan during the Meiji Period (1868–1912). Western foods, for example, bread, espresso, and frozen yogurt gotten well known during the late 20th century.

Another Western impact has been the presentation of timesaving cooking strategies. These incorporate the electric rice cooker, bundled nourishments, for example, moment noodles, moment miso soup, and moment pickling blends. However, the Japanese are as yet dedicated to their exemplary cooking conventions. All foods were divided into five color groups (green, red, yellow, white, and black-purple) and six tastes (bitter, sour, sweet, hot, salty, and delicate). The Japanese continue to use this cooking system.

1.2 History of Traditional Japanese Dishes

Japan is a small country, but each region or even a city has its own specials. Mainly, there is the Kanto region (eastern area of the main island) food and Kansai region (western area of the main island) food. Generally, Kanto food has intense flavours, and Kansai food is lightly seasoned. Many dishes are cooked differently between the Kansai and Kanto regions.

Milk and other dairy items have neglected to appreciate a similar prominence in Europe as they do in Japan. The main Japanese dairy item known to history was delivered between the eighth and fourteenth hundred years. Cattle were often raised only for drawing carts or ploughing fields. To utilize them for meat or even for milk was, until relatively recently, a long-forgotten practice.

Pepper and cloves were known from the eighth century and were imported either by means of China or legitimately from Southeast Asia, and garlic was additionally developed, taking things down a notch. In any case, these flavours were utilized essentially to make medications and beauty care products.

In the absence of red meat, fish was an effective substitute, and as an island nation, this source of food was abundant and has influenced many of today's most famous dishes. However, before the introduction of modern delivery systems, the difficulty of preserving and transporting fresh marine fish minimized consumption in inland areas where freshwater fish were commonly eaten instead.

Preserving fish additionally got famous, and sushi started as a method for saving fish by placing it in boiled rice. Fish that are salted and set-in rice are saved by lactic corrosive maturation, which forestalls the expansion of the microbes that achieve rot. This more established sort of sushi is still delivered in the zones encompassing Lake Biwa in western Japan, and comparative sorts are likewise known in Korea, southwestern China, and Southeast Asia.

To eat Japanese-style suppers, chopsticks are usually utilized. Also, Japanese people use forks, knives, or spoons, depending on what types of food people are eating. The traditional Japanese table setting is to place a bowl of rice on your left and to place a bowl of miso soup on your right side of the table. Other dishes are set behind these bowls. Chopsticks are placed on a chopstick holder in front of soup and rice bowls.

Today, Japanese cooking is still intensely affected by the four seasons and geology. Fish and vegetables are most ordinarily eaten. While to certain westerners, the food may appear to be practically insipid, freshness, presentation, and balance of flavours to be of paramount importance.

1.3 Evolution of Japanese Food over Time

A significant part of the rice devoured by Japan was imported from other Eastern nations, so once the trade stopped, the rice flexibly dwindled. To additional the issue, returnees from combat areas just as U.S. occupation in Japan raised the populace to numbers higher than those of pre-war levels. Helpless rice harvests in 1944 and 1945 because of climate and war compounded the criticalness of the circumstance, bringing about broad hunger and starvation, especially among youngsters.

This suffering, however, ended up having a silver lining. During the U.S. occupation of Japan following World War II, the United States government supplied Japan with large quantities of wheat flour to rehabilitate the Japanese economy as a strategic move during the cold war. This wheat flour served as a substitute for rice, and was used mainly to make wheat noodles for Chinese noodle soup at the time referred to as shina soba or chuka soba. This noodle soup is often sold in Japanese black markets from yatai or small food carts, which later became known as ramen.

The daily diet of the Japanese people has changed drastically over the past years, with corresponding changes in agricultural production. In the early post-war years of food shortage, people ate sweet potatoes, barley, and millet more than white rice, which was scarce and expensive. Vegetables and fish in small quantities served as side dishes.

Although rice regained its traditional place at the centre of the preferred Japanese diet by the early 1950s, western staples of meat, bread, and dairy products soon made inroads. Many people credit the national school lunch program with changing the diet preferences of the younger generation because it served milk and a roll along with a hot dish.

Japanese now eat much more meat, bread, and dairy products, while consumption of rice has declined. By the 1970s, western style restaurants and fast foods further changed the eating habits of urban Japanese. Instead of the traditional diet of rice for breakfast and dinner and noodles for lunch, most urban Japanese now eat a western breakfast and lunch, with rice remaining the staple food only for most dinners.

1.4 Popularity of Japanese Dishes in the U.S.A

Japanese food is getting more mainstream, alongside a developing movement towards sound reasoning. The quantity of Japanese cafés is developing, even in America. While the taste is a reason for the popularity, the colourful plating of items that allow for dishes to also be enjoyed visually is another.

After Italian, Chinese, and Mexican, Japanese food is presumably the most mainstream ethnic cooking in the United States. Before 1970 only a few big cities, and a few Japanese-American communities in Hawaii and California, had Japanese restaurants; the foods, and the manners and customs, attracted few mainstream American diners. The popularity of sushi would change all that. While Americanised sushi variations like the ever-popular California roll made the form popular, once introduced to sushi, Americans began to crave it, even if it meant eating raw fish.

However, real Japanese food is available and popular at restaurants all over the United States of America. Restaurants will, naturally, avoid many Japanese foods that will never appeal to American taste: the pungent, sticky fermented soy paste called natto is a perfect example, although even this is available in Japanese groceries.

A real Japanese restaurant has a staff of Japanese chefs. Good Japanese cooking is subtle and takes a long time to master. Sushi chefs are particularly highly trained and are skilled at avoiding health issues when dealing with raw seafood. A number of pan-Asian restaurants offer Japanese food in combination with Chinese or Korean food. The Japanese dishes at these restaurants should be reliable if prepared by a genuine Japanese chef.

Thirty years ago, the typical Japanese restaurant served a little of everything. Now Japanese food is so popular that the market supports numerous specialties eating concepts such as the famous sushi, tempura, shabu yautia, udon and soba, ramen, teriyaki, bento box, nabe, yakiniku, sukiyaki, and donburi.

Chapter 2: Home Cooking Vs. Dine- in Experience

Japanese cooking incorporates the local and conventional nourishments of Japan, which have created through hundreds of years of political, financial, and social changes. The customary cooking of Japan depends on rice with miso soup and different dishes; there is an emphasis on seasonal ingredients. Side dishes often consist of fish, pickled vegetables, and vegetables cooked in broth.

Seafood is common, often grilled, but also served raw as sashimi or in sushi. Seafood and vegetables are also deep-fried in a light batter, as tempura. Apart from rice, staples include noodles, such as soba and udon. Japan also has many simmered dishes such as fish products in broth called oden, or beef in sukiyaki and nikujaga.

2.1 Difference between Home Cooking Vs. Dine-in Experience

While many restaurants and fast-food outlets offer us convincing marketing statements that they offer healthy and nutritional food, studies frequently find that this is not the case. The sugar and sodium substance of most handled foods cause them to be not kidding dangers to our wellbeing. These are likewise similar characteristics which permit these foods to get addictive. The eatery business supports overconsumption and extravagance in foods that we know to be undesirable for our bodies.

Neither is restaurant food as healthy for us as what we would make at home. At the same time, the cost of eating out puts a large strain on many of our food budgets. Cooking at home is the best choice for having a consistently healthy, budget-friendly diet.

Individuals all around the globe are occupied with work, school and other additional exercises. Nobody actually has the opportunity to cook, so families are continually going out to eat at an eatery. At the point when a family eats at home, they, will pay not as much as cafés in light of the fact that when they purchase food from the market they purchase for better quality and a superior cost. It is very simple. There is most likely even a not insignificant rundown of advantages that a considerable lot of you previously experienced eating at home yourselves. Following are the differences between home cooking and dine-in experience:

1. You can save money.

In the long run, preparing meals at home may save you money. A group of fundamental ingredients frequently comes in at a lower sticker price than a single restaurant dish.

You can likewise wind up getting more suppers out of a formula you make at home than if you request takeout, or have extras to take to work the following day. After only a couple weeks, you could see perceptible reserve funds begin to accumulate.

2. Keep up calorie count.

The average fast food order ranges between 1,100 to 1,200 calories total that is almost all of a woman's recommended daily calorie intake (1,600 to 2,400 calories) and almost two thirds of a man's daily intake (2,000 to 3,000 calories). Furthermore, if you think independent cafés, and modest chains do any better, reconsider. Making a meal yourself means you can make sure the portion sizes and calorie counts are where you want them to be. Recipes often come with nutritional information and serving size suggestions, which makes that even easier.

3. It is fun to cook.

At the point when you are making a meal without any preparation, you will find and explore different avenues regarding various ingredients, flavours, and foods. And as with any activity, the more time you spend in the kitchen, the better you become at creating fantastic meals. You would be missing out this fun if you would keep on ordering your food or going for dine-in to any restaurant.

4. Save plenty of time.

Part of ordering take-out means waiting for the food to arrive or driving to get it. Depending on where you live, what time you order, and whether or not the delivery person is good with directions, this could actually take more time than if you would simply make a meal at home.

Cooking at home does not have to take a lot of time if you do not want it to.

By using different services, you eliminate the need to look for recipes or grocery shop. Everything you need comes right to your door; in the exact pre-portioned amounts you will be using.

5. You will feel healthy

Some research specialists recommend that individuals that more frequently prepare food themselves, instead of getting a take-out meal, have a generally more beneficial eating regimen. These examinations additionally give us the idea that café suppers ordinarily contain higher measures of sodium, immersed fat, absolute fat, and large number of calories than home-prepared meals. While cooking without anyone else at home you have full scale authority over what is going in your food. That can improve things fundamentally to your overall prosperity.

6. More family times.

Cooking together can offer you an event to reconnect with your assistant just as loved ones. Cooking has various favourable circumstances as well. The American Psychological Association communicates that trying new things together like learning another formula together can help keep a couple related and busy with their relationship.

The most important fact is that food simply tastes better when it is been prepared in home rather than any restaurant. Thus, it is smarter to cook home and eat well instead of taking off to an eatery only because of your apathetic daily schedule.

2.2 Health Benefits of Japanese Food

The Japanese eating regimen depends on the rule of wellbeing and life span. Japanese food is not just elegant and mouth-watering yet additionally offers different medical advantages.

Japanese food generally comprises of natural ingredients, refined sugar or other food sources, and high measures of grains and vegetables. Following are a portion of the numerous medical advantages of appreciating Japanese food:

1. Large variety of fruits and vegetables.

The Japanese eating regimen comprises of a wide scope of vegetables, which contains fundamental minerals to help generally sustenance. For instance, kelp is profoundly nutritious, including a lot of iodine that can enable your body to save a sound thyroid. Likewise, high measures of organic product are burned-through for breakfast and treat, which has high measures of fibre and water content.

2. Healthy drinks.

Japanese eateries generally incorporate green tea with their suppers, which have various medical advantages. Green tea is known to help direct pulse, lower glucose, support the safe framework, lower cholesterol, and hinder the maturing cycle. It likewise contains a large portion of the measure of caffeine that espresso does, and assists breaks with bringing down oils in your stomach related framework. Green tea additionally makes a loose and centred mental perspective because of it being wealthy in cancer prevention agents.

3. Reduced risk of various cancers.

Japan has had an extremely low risk for hormone-dependent cancers such as breast and prostate cancers. This is attributed to the high consumption of vegetables, fruits, healthy fats, high-fibre foods, and overall lower calorie intake.

4. Lower chances of cardiac diseases.

Japan has one of the lowest rates for the development of heart disease in the world and even more compared to developed countries. The reasoning behind these low instances of heart diseases is that the Japanese diet is filled with foods that help improve heart health.

Furthermore, Japanese food lacks ingredients in their diet which promotes poor cardiac health like high levels of saturated fats, modified carbohydrates from processed foods, and lower levels of sugar consumption. Soy is commonly in many Japanese dishes, and it is known to decrease the risk of heart attacks, as well as regulate blood pressure. The Japanese use soy as an alternative to red meat, which can be very high in saturated fats.

5. High amount of protein.

The Japanese culture comprehends that eating excellent wellsprings of protein advances a more advantageous way of life. A significant number of the dishes in Japanese food are brimming with protein, which is staggeringly helpful to your body. Fish, chicken, and even tofu are probably the most widely recognized staples in Japanese food. When you eat a lot of protein, you create stronger building blocks for your bones, your muscles, your cartilage, your skin, and even your blood.

Protein also provides large amounts of iron, which keeps your blood oxygenated, so it continues to flow through your body as efficiently as possible. Likewise, the Japanese eating regimen utilizes a ton of fish rather than red meats since it brings down the dangers of coronary episodes. By consuming more fish, you are also gaining a great source of omega 3 fatty acids and brain-boosting nutrients.

The traditional Japanese diet combines simple soups, steamed rice or noodles, fish, seafood, tofu or natto, and a variety of minimally processed sides. The traditional Japanese diet focuses on whole, minimally processed, nutrient-rich, seasonal foods. It is particularly rich in seafood, vegetables, and fruit, and limits meat, dairy, and snacks. It may improve digestion, aid weight management, help you live longer, and protect against various diseases.

2.3 Different Properties of Spices used in Japanese Food

Spices are utilized for flavor and for stylish allure in Japanese cooking. Probably the most widely recognized are: shiso, akajiso, mistuba, kaiware, sancho, and chrysanthemum leaves. Shichimi Togarashi is the most famous flavoring other than soy sauce

1. Mitsuba.

Mitsuba is a tasty kind of parsley with a fresh surface and an invigorating fragrance. Added as an exquisite embellishment to flavorful custard dishes, soups, and sashimi, it is likewise southern style entire in tempura or added to plates of mixed greens. Mitsuba can be utilized at whatever point more grounded tasting parsley is required.

2. Akajiso

Akajiso or red shiso is also used to dye pickled plums red. These umeboshi are used throughout Japanese cuisine as a garnish or as a flavoring in sauces, dressings, rice balls and other dishes. A specialty gin made in Kyoto is made from red shiso and flavoured with yusu, sansho pepper, and juniper berries. This gin which is lighter than its western counterpart has a smooth but complex flavor.

3. Sansho

Sansho is a pretty herb with a dainty balanced design that is a good seasoning for soups and fish dishes, in particular eel specialties or chicken. With its refreshing mint like flavor, sansho is a popular herb enhancer in Japan. Apart from its leaf, the seed pods of the sansho plant give a tingling dimension to eel or chicken dishes; its flavor is lemony and peppery and can deliver a flavorful punch.

4. Yuzu Koshu

Japan's local specialty spice, yuzu kosho, is made of the peel of the Asian citrus yuzu, salt, and chili pepper. You can commonly find it as a tube or jar of yellow paste in Japanese supermarkets. Traditionally used in nabe, or Japanese hotpot, yuzu kosho also pairs wonderfully with miso, tonkatsu (fried pork cutlet), yakitori (grilled meat skewers), sashimi, and all manner of Japanese noodle dishes.

5. Ponzu

Ponzu is the citrus sauce that even those who hate citrus will love. Made from the juice of any citrus fruit, soy sauce, mirin (rice wine), and dashi (Japanese soup stock), this tangy vinaigrette like sauce can brighten the flavor of your gyoza, stir-fry, marinated meats, and tofu dishes.

6. Chrysanthemum

Although somewhat bitter in taste, chrysanthemum leaves are often added to hot pot dishes and stir fries. The buds and flowers are infused to make a celebratory herbal tea served on special occasions like weddings.

7. Wasabi

In case you are acquainted with any topping on this rundown, it is most likely wasabi. Wasabi is notable for being the threateningly hot green glue that goes with sushi, verifiably thought to have restorative properties when eaten with crude fish. Yet, you can likewise utilize it to decorate soba noodles, or even make a wasabi dressing for sushi bowls and cooked fish.

8. Shichimi Togarashi

Shichimi togarashi is a flavorful mixture of sansho, hemp seeds, ground nori, black and white sesame seeds, white poppy seeds, ground chilies, shiso, and ginger and dried tangerine peel. These ingredients vary according to the region, but basically it is a zesty chili powder used to flavor Udon. This popular seven spice seasoning originated in the 1600s when chilies were first introduced to Japan and has been enjoyed ever since as a seasoning for udon, ramen, hot pot, and chicken dishes.

9. Rayu

Commonly found in Japanese-style Chinese food, rayu is chili oil made with sesame oil, garlic, ginger, onion, spices, and sometimes sesame seeds. You may have seen this signature red oil available at the tables of most ramen shops. It also serves as a great dipping sauce for meals and can spice up any regular bowl of rice, noodles, or tofu.

10. Kaiware

Kaiware is a type of radish sprout with a hot, peppery flavor like watercress. Useful as a spicy garnish, it is excellent in sandwiches, stir fries, salads and sushi. Often it is sprinkled on top of tuna or beef tataki to give a peppery accent to the other ingredients.

11. Shiso

Shiso consists of large aromatic leaves, either purple or green, with a refreshing scent and flavor. When served raw with sushi or sashimi, shiso is said to prevent food poisoning because of its antiseptic or antibacterial qualities. Other medicinal characteristics include anti-inflammatory powers with illnesses such as allergies, colds, and arthritis.

Otherwise, shiso leaves are used as a garnish for sashimi, wrapped around onigiri, used to flavor pickled plums, deep fried in tempura batter, or added to rice dishes.

Shiso is also a refreshing herb to add to salads, egg sandwiches, or in sauces such as pesto or gremolata. Very easy to grow in pots on your patio, shiso will grow waist high and propagate easily if the conditions are right.

12.   Furikake

Furikake is a broad term that applies to any dry Japanese spices made to be sprinkled over cooked rice. Common varieties might include salmon flakes, bits of dried omelet, sesame seeds, wasabi, seaweed flakes, bonito flakes, and nearly any other Japanese seasoning you can think of! You can try out special prefectural varieties, or simply stick with safe old seaweed flavor to spice up your rice, noodles, fried chicken, or salads.

13.   Aonori

Aonori, or dried seaweed flakes, are a ubiquitous Japanese seasoning that lends its familiar earthy flavor to much of Japanese cuisine. Traditionally, it goes atop takoyaki, okonomiyaki, and yakisoba.

You will discover a great deal of these fixings in standard Japanese cooking, so unquestionably adventure outside your customary range of familiarity with some conventional and extraordinary Japanese dishes. In any case, the beautiful universe of Japanese flavors and sauces additionally has a lot of space for experimentation.

Chapter 3: Japanese Breakfast Recipes

Rather than the sweet oats or additionally filling bacon and egg dishes that fill in as the cornerstone of numerous American breakfast menus, Japanese morning meals centre on pungent, appetizing flavours that fulfil and empower you for the afternoon.

The components of this hearty-yet-not-too-filling breakfast might seem more like lunch or dinner to Americans, and that is by design.

Following are some amazing Japanese breakfast recipes:

3.1 Japanese Omelette

Cooking Time: 5 minutes

Serving Size: 1

Ingredients:

- Soy sauce, one tbsp.
- Eggs, four
- Sugar, one tbsp.
- Mirin, one tbsp.
- Salt, as required
- Cooking oil, as required

Method:

1. First, beat your eggs well in a bowl using either a fork, or chopsticks if you are an expert chopstick user.

2. Add one tablespoon each of soy sauce, mirin and sugar and a little salt to your mix.

3. Put a small amount of cooking oil in your pan and bring it up to medium heat. Keep some kitchen roll handy to help keep the pan oiled during cooking.

4. Add a small amount of your egg mix into the heated pan. Once the egg is cooked slightly so that the top is still slightly uncooked, push it over to the side of your pan.

5. Add a little more oil to the pan using the kitchen roll and add another small amount of the egg mix to your pan.

6. You can then begin to roll the first bit of egg over the mix you just put in the pan until you have a small roll of egg.

7. Continue adding a small amount of egg while oiling the pan each time in between.

8. Your omelette is now done so remove from the pan and wait to cool before slicing it up into thin pieces with a sharp knife.

9. Your dish is ready to be served.

3.2 Breakfast Ramen

Cooking Time: 25 minutes

Serving Size: 6

Ingredients:

- Sage leaves, a bunch
- Unsalted butter, a quarter cup
- Bacon, eight strips
- Enki mushrooms, a bunch
- Miso soup, two cups
- Broth, twelve cups
- Poached eggs, six
- Ramen noodles, six cups
- Tomato, one
- Salt, as required
- Cooking oil, as required
- Avocado, one

Method:

1. Preheat oven to 400 degrees. Lay a piece of parchment paper on a baking sheet.

2. Spread the bacon strips on the sheet and bake for about twenty minutes. Watch carefully as time

will vary with ovens. They will crisp up with no need to turn the pieces over. Save your bacon grease in a jar because you can use it to make the ramen soup bases. Remove from the oven and set on a paper towel.

3. Heat the butter in a small skillet over high heat until the butter starts to brown. Immediately scatter the sage leaves in the pan and cook for about 10 seconds.

4. Boil a pot of water for your noodles. In a separate saucepan, bring two cups miso base, and twelve cups (2.8 L) of broth to a boil, then lower the heat and let it simmer until it is ready to be served.

5. Boil the noodles. If fresh, boil for about one minute, if packaged, boil for about two minutes. As soon as they are done, drain well and separate into serving bowls.

6. Pour two cups of soup over each bowl of noodles.

7. Top each bowl with mushrooms, avocado slices, tomatoes, poached egg, a crumbled up half strip of bacon, and crispy sage; lay another whole piece of bacon on the side.

8. Drizzle the browned butter over the top for added flavour.

9. You dish is ready to be served.

3.3 Japanese Style Pancakes

Cooking Time: 40 minutes

Serving Size: 4

Ingredients:

- Milk, one and a half cup
- Baking powder, two tsp.
- Sugar, three tbsp.
- Kosher salt, half tsp.
- Unsalted butter, four tbsp.
- Eggs, four
- Vanilla extract, one tsp.
- Cream of tartar, a quarter tsp.
- Maple syrup, as required
- All-purpose flour, one and a half cup

Method:

1. Whisk together the flour, sugar, baking powder and salt in a large bowl.

2. Whisk together the milk, melted butter, vanilla and egg yolk in a medium bowl until combined.

3. Beat the egg whites and cream of tartar in another large bowl with an electric mixer on medium-high speed until stiff peaks form, about two minutes.

4. Stir the milk mixture into the flour mixture until just combined. Then gently fold in the remaining egg whites until just combined.

5. Coat a large non-stick skillet with non-stick cooking spray and heat over medium-low heat.

6. Put the prepared ring moulds in the middle of the skillet and fill each with half cup of batter.

7. Cover the skillet with the lid and cook until the batter rises to the tops of the ring moulds and is golden on the bottom for about five minutes.

8. Release the bottom of the pancakes with a spatula. Grasp the sides of the ring moulds with tongs to stabilize them and then carefully flip.

9. Cover and cook until golden on the other side, about five minutes more. Transfer to a plate and remove the mould.

10. Serve with butter and maple syrup.

3.4 Japanese Breakfast Rice Bowl

Cooking Time: 3 minutes

Serving Size: 1

Ingredients:

- Egg, one
- Thinly sliced nori, as required
- Hondashi, a pinch
- Mirin, half tsp.
- Soy sauce, half tsp.
- MSG, a pinch
- Furikake, as required
- Cooked white rice, one cup

Method:

1. Place rice in a bowl and make a shallow scoop in the centre.
2. Break the whole egg into the centre.
3. Season with half teaspoon soy sauce, a pinch of salt, a pinch of MSG, half teaspoon mirin, and a pinch of Hondashi.
4. Stir vigorously with chopsticks to incorporate egg; it should become pale yellow, frothy, and fluffy in texture.
5. Taste and adjust seasonings as necessary.
6. Sprinkle with furikake and nori, make a small scoop in the top, and add the other egg yolk.
7. Your dish is ready to be served.

3.5 Tamagoyaki

Cooking Time: 10 minutes

Serving Size: 2

Ingredients:

- Eggs, three
- Olive oil, one tsp.
- Shirodashi, two tsp.
- Salt, pinch
- Water, two tbsp.

Method:

1. Crack the eggs into a medium size mixing bowl.
2. Add seasoning and mix them all together gently to avoid too much bubble forming.
3. Strain the egg mixture through a sieve a few times.
4. Pour about two tbsp. oil in a small bowl and soak kitchen paper and set aside.
5. Heat two tsp. olive oil in the frying pan over medium heat till you can feel the heat when you hover your hand over the pan.
6. Pour a quarter of egg mixture into the pan.
7. Break any bubbles that have been formed with the edge of the chopsticks and scramble gently and slightly.
8. When the surface is solidified a little, fold and push the egg to one end of the pan with chopsticks.

9. Repeat the procedure and make an egg roll.

10. Your dish is ready to be served.

3.6 Tonkatsu

Cooking Time: 10 minutes

Serving Size: 4

Ingredients:

- Eggs, two
- Flour, as required
- Tonkatsu sauce, for serving
- Shredded Napa cabbage, as required
- Bread crumbs, as required
- Pork loins, four pieces
- Oil, for frying
- Salt, pinch
- Pepper, as required

Method:

1. Pound to flatten the loin cutlet to about a quarter inch. Salt and pepper both sides of each cutlet.

2. Dredge each in flour, then dip into beaten eggs and press into bread crumbs to coat both sides.

3. Heat a large skillet with about half inch of oil until hot.

4. Lay the cutlets in the hot oil. Deep-fry until golden brown, about five minutes, turning them once or twice.

5. Drain the cutlets on paper towels and cut the pork into bite-size strips that can be eaten with chopsticks.

6. Arrange the pork on a platter lined with the shredded cabbage, and garnish with lemon wedges.

7. Serve the sauce on the side for dipping, or pour it over the pork and cabbage.

3.7 Japanese Egg Omelette Sandwich

Cooking Time: 5 minutes

Serving Size: 2

Ingredients:

- Eggs, two
- Japanese soup stock, half tsp.
- Hot water, one tsp.
- Soy sauce, one tsp.
- Mayonnaise, as required
- Bread slices, four
- Oil, for frying
- Salt, pinch
- Pepper, as required

Method:

1. Melt the Japanese soup stock in hot water, and keep it cool.

2. Mix all ingredients using a whisk.

3. Put oil thinly to a 12 cm × 12 cm heat-resistant container.

4. Wrap the container and warm one minute thirty seconds with microwave.

5. Take it out and keep it cool. Wipe off extra moisture with kitchen paper.

6. Spread the mayonnaise over one side of breads. Put on omelette and cut it into four pieces.

7. Your dish is ready to be served.

3.8 Japanese Rolled Omelette

Cooking Time: 10 minutes

Serving Size: 4

Ingredients:

- Eggs, six
- Daikon, for serving
- Soy sauce, one tsp.
- Salt, one tsp.
- Mirin, one tbsp.
- Caster sugar, one tbsp.
- Shiso leaves, as required
- Oil, for frying

Method:

1. Mix the dashi stock with mirin, sugar, soy sauce, and salt.

2. Add to the beaten eggs and stir well. Heat the omelette pan over medium heat.

3. Pour in some egg mixture and tilt the pan to coat evenly.

4. When the omelette starts to set, roll it up towards you, using a pair of chopsticks or a spatula.

5. Keep the rolled omelette in the pan and push it back to the farthest side from you.

6. Again, pour in some egg mixture into the empty side, lift up the first roll with chopsticks and let the egg mixture runs underneath.

7. When it looks half set, roll the omelette around the first roll to make a single roll with many layers.

8. Repeat the process until all egg mixture is used up.

9. Move the roll gently onto a sushi rolling mat covered with a clear sheet of plastic wrap.

10. Roll the omelette firmly into the mat and leave to sushi rolled for five minutes.

11. Grate the daikon with a daikon grater or with a very fine grater.

12. Cut the rolled omelette into one-inch slices crossways. Lay the shiso leaves on a plate and place a few pieces of omelette on top.

13. Put a small heap of grated daikon to one side and add and serve.

3.9 Hiroshima Okonomiyaki

Cooking Time: 30 minutes

Serving Size: 2

Ingredients:

- Water, two tbsps.

- Eggs, three

- Bacon, six strips

- Cabbage, 150g

- Okonomiyaki flour, half cup

- Okonomiyaki sauce, two tbsp.

- Spring onions, as required

- Bonito flakes, as required

- Yakisoba noodles, two cups

- Pickled ginger, one tsp.

- Oil, for frying

- Aonori seaweed, as required

Method:

1. Begin by chopping your green onion and cabbage. Try to chop your cabbage as finely as possible.

2. Grab a bowl and mix the okonomiyaki flour with the water, and one egg until you have a smooth batter with no lumps.

3. Now the fun part, take a frying pan or hot plate, and grease with a splash of vegetable oil and place on a medium heat.

4. Make sure the pan is evenly heated before the next step or the okonomiyaki will be difficult to be shaped.

5. Add just under half the batter to the pan in a nice even circle, remember not to make the circle too wide otherwise it will not be able to keep its shape.

6. Next, add half of the cabbage and half of the bean sprouts on top of the batter, before adding a layer of bacon.

7. Pour one tbsp. of the batter on the top of the mix to hold everything together and let the okonomiyaki cook for about ten minutes before flipping it over with a spatula to cook on the other side.

8. Grab another pan and cook one serving of yakisoba with a bit of vegetable oil and the sauce provided in the packet.

9. Once the yakisoba is cooked, with a spatula move the okonomiyaki on top of the noodles.

10. Crack an egg in a bowl and break the yolk before pouring in the first pan to the side of the okonomiyaki.

11. Place the okonomiyaki over the egg and leave to cook for two minutes.

12. Once done, flip the completed okonomiyaki over onto a plate and smother in a criss-cross pattern with okonomiyaki sauce and mayonnaise.

13. The final touch is to sprinkle the spring onion, aonori seaweed, katsuobushi and pickled ginger on the top.

3.10 Japanese Hibachi Style Fried Rice

Cooking Time: 20 minutes

Serving Size: 4

Ingredients:

- Toasted sesame oil, one tbsp.
- Salt, as required
- Ground black pepper, as required
- Eggs, two
- Cooked rice, four cups
- Soy sauce, two tbsp.
- Chopped onion, one
- Butter, four tbsp.

Method:

1. Heat a wok or large skillet over medium-high heat.

2. In a small bowl, lightly whisk together the eggs, salt, and ground black pepper.

3. Add one tablespoon of butter into the heated wok or skillet. Once the butter melts, add in the eggs and scramble until they are no longer thin but still a soft scramble.

4. Carefully remove the cooked eggs from the skillet or wok back into the small bowl. Set aside.

5. Add in another one tablespoon of butter into the heated wok or skillet. Once the butter melts, add in the chopped onion and move around in the pan until the onion is lightly coated with the butter. Allow the onion to continue to cook until it becomes translucent.

6. Add in the remaining two tablespoons of butter into the wok or skillet along with the cooked onion. Once it melts add in the cooked rice.

7. Add in the soy sauce and toasted sesame oil with the rice. Stir the rice frequently, breaking it up as needed. Once the fried rice has been heated thoroughly and has also lightly browned, add in the egg and stir to evenly distribute.

8. Serve warm with some yum sauce.

3.11 Japanese Breakfast Skillet

Cooking Time: 20 minutes

Serving Size: 2

Ingredients:

- Japanese sweet potato, half cup
- Sliced carrots, half cup
- Fresh ginger, half tsp.
- Mirin, a quarter cup
- Sliced mushrooms, one cup
- Tamari, two tbsp.
- White onions, half cup
- Sesame oil, two tbsp.
- Organic tempeh, one block
- Vegetable broth, two cups

Method:

1. In a medium pot that will fit the block of tempeh, combine the tempeh and the vegetable broth and bring to a boil.

2. Immediately reduce to heat and simmer gently for fifteen minutes. When done, dice into small cubes and set aside.

3. In a large skillet, warm the oil and then add the diced potatoes and sliced carrots. Adjust heat to medium high and cook for fifteen minutes until the vegetables have a nice, golden color to them.

4. Add in the onions and tempeh and continue sautéing for about three minutes.

5. Add the cabbage, garlic, ginger and mushrooms, then give it a quick stir. The pan should be very dry.

6. Now deglaze with the mirin and tamari.

7. Stir for a few minutes to coat everything in the glaze.

8. Your dish is ready to be.served.

All the recipes mentioned above are very easy to make at home.

Chapter 4: Japanese Lunch and Dinner Recipes

If you are an accomplished home cook or new to cooking, Japanese food is a delectable food to prepare at home. This rundown of essential Japanese plans is an extraordinary beginning stage for learning to cook all by yourself. It is useful to know the Japanese food technique. When you ace these, you can go for more complicated plans and procedures.

4.1 Onigiri

Cooking Time: 20 minutes

Serving Size: 3

Ingredients:

- Nori sheet, as required
- Umeboshi, one
- Soy sauce, half tsp.
- Mirin, half tsp.
- Tuna, one cup
- Japanese mayonnaise, two tbsp.
- Salted salmon, one piece
- Cooked rice, two cups

Method:

1. Cook the rice according to your rice cooker or if you do not have a rice cooker, follow the instructions here.

2. Transfer the cooked rice to a separate bowl to cool it down.

3. Prepare all the fillings that you are going to use and set aside.

4. Prepare seaweed sheet.

5. Place cling wrap over a rice bowl.

6. Place some of the cooked rice over the centre of the cling wrap.

7. Put about 1tsp of umeboshi on the centre of the rice then cover with the rice around.

8. Wrap the cling wrap over the rice and squeeze and mould the rice into a triangle shape with your hands.

9. Remove the cling wrap and cover the bottom of the rice triangle with a nori sheet.

10. Your dish is ready to be served.

4.2 Natto

Cooking Time: 20 minutes

Serving Size: 1

Ingredients:

- Scallions, for garnish
- Natto, one tbsp.
- Soy sauce, half tsp.
- Saikkyo, one and a half tsp.
- Tofu, half block
- Miso, two tbsp.
- Wakame seeds, a handful
- Dashi, two cups

Method:

1. Bring the dashi to a simmer in a soup pot and place the spoonful of natto into the liquid. Simmer for two minutes.

2. Place the miso pastes into the pot and use the back of a spoon to dissolve the pastes into the dashi.

3. Add the wakame and the tofu and simmer for 30 seconds longer.

4. Garnish with scallions.

5. Serve immediately.

4.3 Agedashi Tofu

Cooking Time: 20 minutes

Serving Size: 3

Ingredients:

- Flavoured oil, three cups
- Corn starch, four tbsp.
- Soy sauce, two tbsp.
- Katsuobishi, as required
- Tofu, one block
- Mirin, two tbsp.
- Daikon radish, as required
- Scallions, as required
- Shichimi Togarashi, a handful
- Dashi, one cup

Method:

1. Gather all the ingredients.

2. Wrap the tofu with three layers of paper towels and place another plate on top. Drain the water out of tofu for fifteen minutes.

3. Peel and grate the daikon and gently squeeze water out. Cut the green onion into thin slices.

4. Put dashi, soy sauce, and mirin in a small saucepan and bring to boil.

5. Remove the tofu from paper towels and cut it into eight pieces.

6. Coat the tofu with potato starch, leaving excess flour, and immediately deep fry until they turn light brown and crispy.

7. Remove the tofu and drain excess oil on a plate lined with paper towels or wire rack.

8. To serve, place the tofu in a serving bowl and gently pour the sauce without wetting the tofu.

9. Garnish with grated daikon, green onion, katsuobushi, and shichimi togarashi.

4.4 Nasu Dengaku

Cooking Time: 30 minutes

Serving Size: 4

Ingredients:
- Japanese eggplant, three
- Flavoured oil, one tbsp.
- Sake, two tbsp.
- Sugar, two tbsp.
- Miso, four tbsp.
- Sesame seeds, as required

- Tofu, one block
- Mirin, two tbsp.
- Daikon radish, three
- Konnyaku, a handful

Method:

1. Combine sake, mirin, sugar, and miso in a saucepan.
2. Mix well to combine and then bring to a gentle simmer over the lowest heat. Stir constantly and cook for few minutes.
3. When the miso is thickened, it is ready to use.
4. Use the miso glaze to slather on the foods you prepare below.
5. Wrap the tofu with two sheets of paper towel and press the tofu between two plates for 30 minutes.
6. Once the tofu is dried, cut it into small bite-sized pieces.
7. Cut the eggplant in half lengthwise and cut it in a crisscross pattern. This will help the eggplant absorb more flavors.
8. Immediately soak in water to prevent the eggplants from changing colors, and to remove the bitter taste. Drain and dry with a paper towel.
9. Place the tofu and eggplants on a rimmed baking sheet lined with parchment paper or silicone baking sheet. With a brush, apply vegetable oil on top and bottom of tofu and eggplants.
10. Bake at 400 degrees for twenty minutes, or until the eggplant is tender. Transfer the baking sheet to the working surface.

11.   Meanwhile, carefully spoon some of the miso glaze onto your tofu and eggplants and spread evenly. Broil for five minutes, or until the top has nice char and caramelization.

12.   Transfer to a serving platter, sprinkle with sesame seeds and serve immediately.

4.5 Omurice

Cooking Time: 20 minutes

Serving Size: 2

Ingredients:

- Boneless chicken, one pound
- Olive oil, one tbsp.
- Mixed vegetables, half cup
- Salt and pepper, as required
- Cooked Japanese rice, one and a half cup
- Soy sauce, one tsp.
- Ketchup, one tbsp.
- Milk, two tbsp.
- Eggs, two
- Cheese, a handful

Method:

1. Gather all the ingredients.
2. Chop the onion finely.
3. Cut the chicken.
4. Heat the oil in a non-stick pan and sauté the onion until softened.
5. Add the chicken and cook until no longer pink.
6. Add the mixed vegetables and season with salt and pepper.
7. Add the rice and break into small pieces.
8. Add ketchup and soy sauce and combine everything evenly with a spatula. Transfer the fried rice to a plate and wash the pan.

9. We will make the omelette one at a time. Whisk the egg and milk in a small bowl.

10.   Heat the olive oil in the pan over medium high heat.

11.   When the pan is hot, pour the egg mixture into the pan and tilt to cover the bottom of the pan. Lower the heat when the bottom of the egg is set.

12.   Put the cheese and the divided fried rice on top of the omelette.

13.   Use the spatula to fold both sides of omelette toward the middle to cover the fried rice. Slowly move the omurice to the edge of the pan.

14.   Hold a plate in one hand and the pan in the other hand flip the pan and move the omurice to the plate.

15.   While it is still hot, cover the omurice with a paper towel and shape it. Drizzle the ketchup on top for decoration.

4.6 Okonomiyaki

Cooking Time: 30 minutes

Serving Size: 4

Ingredients:

- Dashi, one cup
- Oyster sauce, one tbsp.
- Nagaimo, as required
- Salt, as required
- Flour one and a half cup
- Sugar, half tsp.
- Baking powder, half tsp.
- Sliced pork belly, half pound
- Milk, two tbsp.
- Eggs, four
- Cabbage, one

Method:

1. Mix all the batter ingredients.
2. Peel and grate nagaimo in a small bowl.
3. Add the grated nagaimo and dashi in the bowl.
4. Mix all together till combined. Cover the bowl with plastic wrap and let it rest in the refrigerator for at least an hour.
5. Cut the pork belly slices in half and set aside.
6. Take out the batter from the refrigerator and add eggs, tempura scraps, and pickled red ginger in the bowl. Mix well until well-combined.
7. Add chopped cabbage to the batter. Mix well before adding the rest.

8. In a large pan, heat vegetable oil on medium heat. Spread the batter evenly. If you are new to making okonomiyaki, make a smaller and thinner size so it is easier to flip.

9. Place the sliced pork belly on top of Okonomiyaki and cook covered for five minutes.

10. Gently press the okonomiyaki to fix the shape and keep it together. Cover and cook for another five minutes.

11. Flip over one last time and cook uncovered for two minutes. If you are going to cook next batch, transfer to a plate.

12. Serve with your preferred toppings.

4.7 Cheesy Ramen Carbonara

Cooking Time: 30 minutes

Serving Size: 4

Ingredients:

- Dashi, one cup
- Olive oil, one tbsp.
- Bacon slices, six
- Salt, as required
- Minced garlic, two
- Parsley, as required
- Parmesan cheese, half cup
- Milk, two tbsp.
- Eggs, two
- Ramen pack, three

Method:

1. Combine all the ingredients.

2. Boil noodles according to package instructions.

3. Save a quarter cup of cooking water to loosen sauce later, if needed. Drain noodles and toss with olive oil so that they do not stick.

4. Heat medium skillet over medium heat. Cook bacon pieces until brown and crisp. Add the noodles to the skillet and toss with the bacon until the noodles are coated in the bacon fat.

5. Beat eggs with fork and mix in parmesan cheese. Pour egg-cheese mixture to skillet and toss with bacon and noodles.

6. Divide between bowls. Garnish with parsley and freshly ground pepper.

4.8 Yakisoba

Cooking Time: 30 minutes

Serving Size: 4

Ingredients:

- Fish sauce, two tbsp.
- Egg, one
- Soy sauce, half cup
- Cooked Japanese rice, three cups
- Tomatoes, two
- Cilantro, half cup
- Salt and pepper, to taste
- Vegetable oil, two tbsp.
- Japanese chili peppers, three
- Toasted walnuts, half cup
- Chicken breast, eight ounces
- Onion, one
- Scallions, half cup
- Minced garlic, one tsp.

Instructions:

1. Heat a large nonstick pan over high heat.
2. Meanwhile, season chicken lightly with salt and pepper.
3. When the wok is very hot, add two tsp of the oil.
4. When the oil is hot, add the chicken and cook on high until it is browned all over and cooked through.

5. Remove chicken   and set aside, add the eggs, pinch of salt and cook a minute or two until done.

6. Add the remaining oil to the wok and add the onion, scallions and garlic.

7. Sauté for a minute, add the chili pepper if using, tomatoes and stir in all the rice.

8. Add the soy sauce and fish sauce stir to mix all the ingredients.

9. Keep stirring a few minutes, and then add egg and chicken back to the wok.

10.   Adjust soy sauce if needed and stir well for another 30 seconds.

11.   Your dish is ready to be served.

4.9 Baked chicken Katsu

Cooking Time: 25 minutes

Serving Size: 4

Ingredients:

- Boneless chicken breast pieces, one pound
- Panko, one cup
- All-purpose flour, half cup
- Water, one tbsp.
- Egg, one
- Salt and pepper, to taste
- Tonkatsu sauce, as required

Instructions:

1. Gather all the ingredients. Adjust an oven rack to the middle position and preheat the oven to 400 degrees. Line a rimmed baking sheet with parchment paper.

2. Combine the panko and oil in a frying pan and toast over medium heat until golden brown. Transfer panko into a shallow dish and allow to cool down.

3. Butterfly the chicken breast and cut in half. Using a mallet or rolling pin, pound the chicken to equal thickness if necessary. Season salt and pepper on both sides of the chicken.

4. In a shallow dish, add flour and in another shallow dish, whisk together the egg and water.

5. Coat each chicken piece in the flour and shake off any excess flour. Dip into the egg mixture and then coat with the toasted panko, pressing firmly to adhere to the chicken.

6. Place the chicken pieces on the prepared baking sheet for about twenty minutes. Serve immediately or transfer to a wire rack so the bottom of the katsu does not get soggy from the moisture.

7. Serve with salad and tonkatsu sauce on the side.

4.10 Hayashi Ground Beef Curry

Cooking Time: 15 minutes

Serving Size: 2

Ingredients:

- Onion, one
- Carrots, half cup
- Ground beef, half pound
- Canola oil, one tbsp.
- Ketchup, two tbsp.
- Salt and pepper, to taste
- Corn starch, one tsp.
- Beef broth, one cup
- Sake, one tbsp.
- Boiled egg, one
- Worcestershire sauce, one tbsp.

Instructions:

1. Slice onion half. One half will be for frying; the other will go in with the dry curry.

2. Slice one half into thin half-moons. Finely chop the other one.

3. Boil egg and cut into small pieces or mash with a fork. Season well with salt and pepper.

4. Heat oil and add onions and carrots.

5. Sprinkle corn starch on top of ground beef and add to the vegetables. Add a quarter cup beef broth and break the ground beef while stirring.

6. Add beef broth, ketchup, sake, and Worcestershire sauce.

7. Mix well and cook for ten minutes or until all the liquid has evaporated. Season with salt and pepper.

8. Fry onions in a separate pan until crispy.

9. Put rice on a plate, top with curry, eggs and fried onions.

4.11 Ramen Noodle Skillet with Steak

Cooking Time: 15 minutes

Serving Size: 2

Ingredients:

- Onion, one
- Carrots, half cup
- Ground beef, half pound
- Canola oil, one tbsp.
- Ketchup, two tbsp.
- Salt and pepper, to taste
- Corn starch, one tsp.
- Beef broth, one cup
- Sake, one tbsp.
- Boiled egg, one
- Worcestershire sauce, one tbsp.

Instructions:

1. In a large skillet over medium-high heat, heat oil.

2. Add steak and sear until your desired completion, about five minutes per side for medium, then transfer to a cutting board and let it rest for five minutes, and then slice it.

3. In a small bowl, whisk together soy sauce, garlic, lime juice, honey, and cayenne until combined and set aside.

4. Add onion, peppers, and broccoli to skillet and cook until tender, then add soy sauce mixture and stir until fully coated.

5. Add cooked ramen noodles and steak and toss until combined.

6. Your dish is ready to be served.

4.12 Chicken Teriyaki

Cooking Time: 15 minutes

Serving Size: 2

Ingredients:

- Sesame oil, one tsp.
- Broccoli, for serving
- Honey, one tbsp.
- Ketchup, two tbsp.
- Salt and pepper, to taste
- Corn starch, one tsp.
- Cooked white rice, one cup
- Garlic and ginger, one tbsp.
- Boiled egg, one
- Soy sauce, one tbsp.

Instructions:

1. In a medium bowl, whisk together soy sauce, rice vinegar, oil, honey, garlic, ginger, and corn starch.

2. In a large skillet over medium heat, heat oil. Add chicken to skillet and season with salt and pepper. Cook until golden and almost cooked through.

3. Cover chicken and simmer until sauce is thickened slightly and chicken is cooked through.

4. Garnish with sesame seeds and green onions.

5. Serve over rice with steamed broccoli.

4.13 Japanese Salmon Bowl

Cooking Time: 30 minutes

Serving Size: 4

Ingredients:

- Chili sauce, one tsp.
- Soy sauce, one tsp.
- Rice, two cups
- Sesame oil, one tbsp.
- Ginger, two tbsp.
- Salt and pepper, to taste
- Sesame seeds, one tsp.
- Vinegar, one tsp.
- Shredded nori, as required
- Salmon, half pound
- Shredded cabbage, one cup

Instructions:

1. Place the rice, three cups of water and half teaspoon of salt in a large pot and bring to the boil.

2. Reduce the heat to low, place the lid on top and cook for fifteen minutes or until water is absorbed.

3. Remove from heat and let stand covered for five minutes.

4. Place the vinegar, soy sauce, chilli sauce, sesame oil, sesame seeds and ginger in a bowl and mix well.

5. Add the salmon and gently stir until completely coated.

6. Place the shredded cabbage and sesame oil in a bowl and mix until well combined.

7. Place a large spoonful of rice in each bowl, add the cabbage and squeeze over the mayonnaise.

8. Garnish with toasted shredded nori and toasted sesame seeds.

Cooking Time: 30 minutes

Serving Size: 4

Ingredients:

- Japanese rice, two cups
- Rice vinegar, a quarter cup
- Salt, one tsp.
- Sugar, two tbsp.
- Shitake mushrooms, eight
- Sashimi, half pound
- Eggs, three
- Mirin, one tsp.
- Sesame seeds, as required
- Tuna, half pound

Instructions:

1. Combine the ingredients.

2. Put rice in a large bowl and wash it with cold water. Repeat washing until the water becomes almost clear. Drain the rice in a colander and set aside for thirty minutes.

3. Place the rice in a rice cooker and add about two cups of water. Let the rice soak in the water for at least thirty minutes. Start the cooker.

4. In a small saucepan, mix rice vinegar, sugar, and salt. Put the pan on low heat and heat until the sugar dissolves. Cool the vinegar mixture.

5. Spread the hot steamed rice into a large plate or a large bowl. Sprinkle the vinegar mixture over the rice and quickly mix into the rice using a shamoji.

6. Meanwhile, remove stems from shiitake and slice thinly. Heat half cup of the reserved water used for rehydrating shiitake in a medium pan.

7. Add shiitake, soy sauce, sugar, and mirin. Simmer shiitake on low heat until the liquid is almost gone.

8. Make the omelettes by beating eggs in a bowl with sugar.

9. Oil a medium skillet and pour a scoop of egg mixture and make a thin omelette.

10. Serve sushi rice on a large plate or individual bowls.

11. Spread simmered shiitake, cucumber, imitation crab meat, and omelette strips over rice. Place tuna sashimi on top. Garnish with sesame seeds.

4.15 Broiled Shrimp and Vegetables/ Kushiyaki

Cooking Time: 10 minutes

Serving Size: 4

Ingredients:

- Lime juice, three tbsp.
- Shrimp, two pounds
- Salt and pepper, to taste
- Chili, one tbsp.
- Mix vegetables, one cup
- Sashimi, half pound
- Eggs, three
- Mirin, one tsp.
- Sesame seeds, as required

Instructions:

1. Marinate the shrimp with the spices, lime juice and olive oil.
2. Meanwhile, chop and slice the veggies.
3. Add one tablespoon of olive oil in a skillet and bring to medium heat.
4. Sauté the veggies until they obtain a golden colour and are tender. Remove and set aside in a bowl.
5. In the same skillet, sauté the shrimp until they are fully cooked. Then return the cookies veggies to the skillet, and sauté with the shrimps for two minutes.
6. Remove and serve.

4.16 Chicken in a Pot/Mizutaki

Cooking Time: 10 minutes

Serving Size: 4

Ingredients:

- Negi, one
- Mizuna, four
- Napa cabbage, eight
- Carrot, half cup
- Chicken thighs, one pound
- Kombu, half pound
- Sake, one tsp.
- Ginger, one tsp.
- Sesame seeds, as required

Instructions:

1. Mix all the ingredients.
2. In a large bowl, add five cups of water, and kombu to make cold brew kombu dashi. Set aside while you prepare the chicken.
3. Fill a medium pot with water and add the bone-in, skin-on chicken thigh pieces. Turn the heat on medium-low.
4. Bring the water to a boil and cook for one minute and discard the water.
5. Rinse the chicken, especially around the bone area, under lukewarm water.
6. In the cold brew kombu dashi, add the chicken thigh pieces you just rinsed.
7. Also add the chicken pieces sake, and ginger.

8. Bring it to a boil over medium heat.

9. Reduce the heat to medium-low and cook covered for thirty minutes. During this time, start preparing other ingredients. After thirty minutes, remove and discard the ginger slices.

10.   Your dish is ready to be served.

Chapter 5: Japanese Salad Recipes

Regardless of the season, most Japanese meals are served with a salad to keep things in balance. A well-composed salad refreshes your palate, provides a pop of colour, and its crisp flavours enhance everything else on the table.

5.1 Japanese cucumber Salad (Sunomo)

Cooking Time: 10 minutes

Serving Size: 8

Ingredients:

- Peanuts, half cup
- Soy sauce, three tbsp.
- Sesame oil, one tsp.
- Sugar, one tbsp.
- Wine vinegar, three tbsp.
- Small cucumber, twelve ounces
- Garlic, one
- Fresh cilantro, as required

Instructions:

1. Whisk the dressing together and be sure to taste it to adjust anything you like.
2. Finely grind the peanuts in a food processor using the pulsing button. You want them to be very fine but be careful not to go too far and turn them into peanut butter.
3. Thinly slice the cucumbers in the diagonal shape.

4. If you would like to remove part of the peel first, you can run a zesting tool down the sides, or simply run the tines of a fork down the sides to create a decorative edge.

5. Put the cucumbers in a bowl and toss with enough dressing to coat thoroughly, you may not need all of it.

6. Toss with the crushed peanuts, sprinkle with chili flakes, and top with cilantro leaves.

7. Serve immediately or chill until ready to serve.

5.2 Japanese Watercess Salad

Cooking Time: 10 minutes

Serving Size: 2

Ingredients:

- Peanut butter, three tbsp.

- Rice vinegar, one tbsp.

- Honey, one tsp.

- Sugar, one tbsp.

- Wine vinegar, three tbsp.

- Watercress, six cups

- Mirin, two tbsp.

Instructions:

1. In a medium size pot, bring water, salted with one tablespoon kosher salt, to boil.

2. Put the peanut butter, honey, rice vinegar, soy sauce, and mirin in a medium bowl.

3. Rinse the watercress, drain and separate the leaves from the stems.

4. Roughly chop the stems and add to the boiling water along with the leaves.

5. Cook until the stems are tender but yielding a soft crunch.

6. Drain, rinse under cold water and softly squeeze out excess water.

7. Gently pat the watercress, dry with a paper towel and add to a mixing bowl.

8. Pour the dressing over the watercress and toss until the watercress is evenly coated.

5.3 Kani Salad

Cooking Time: 10 minutes

Serving Size: 4

Ingredients:

- Carrot, one medium
- Cucumber, two medium sized
- Ripe mango, one cup
- Japanese mayonnaise, one tbsp.
- Half lemon
- Salt and pepper to taste
- Kani, 150 g

Instructions:

1. Peel the carrots and trim off the ends.

2. Do the same with the cucumber but do not include the core with seeds.

3. Shred the crab sticks by hand by gently pressing a piece from end to end to loosen the strips and then separate each strip from one another.

4. Peel the ripe mango.

5. In a large bowl, add the cucumber, carrots, Kani, mango and Japanese mayo. Squeeze the juices of half a lemon on top and toss.

6. Season with salt and pepper as needed, and give it another toss until all ingredients are well blended.

7. Serve immediately or refrigerate until ready.

8. Serve on top of a layer of iceberg or romaine lettuce.

5.4 Oshitashi

Cooking Time: 5 minutes

Serving Size: 1

Ingredients:

- Spinach, one pound
- Sesame seeds, one tbsp.
- Soy sauce, one tbsp.
- Mirin, one tbsp.

Instructions:

1. Toast the sesame seeds in a skillet until lightly coloured.

2. Add the spinach to a large saucepan of boiling water and cook two to three minutes until wilted.

3. Have an ice bath ready.

4. Drain the spinach in a colander.

5. Squeeze dry and place in a bowl.

6. Mix the cooked spinach with the soy sauce, mirin and sesame seeds.

7. Serve at room temperature.

5.5 Japanese Cabbage Salad

Cooking Time: 5 minutes

Serving Size: 1

Ingredients:

- Coleslaw mix, one cup
- Sesame seeds, one tbsp.
- Soy sauce, one tbsp.
- Mirin, one tbsp.
- Bonito flakes, as required

Instructions:

1. Mix all the ingredients for the dressing together in a bowl and pour it over the shredded coleslaw mix.
2. Toss well and top with sesame seeds and bonito flakes.

5.6 Ramen Noodle Salad

Cooking Time: 15 minutes

Serving Size: 1

Ingredients:

- Cabbage and onion, one cup
- Sesame seeds, one tbsp.
- Soy sauce, one tbsp.

- Sugar, one tbsp.
- Vinegar, one tbsp.
- Butter, as required
- Ramen noodles, one pack
- Almonds, as required

Instructions:

1. Combine the oil, vinegar, sugar, and soy sauce in a jar and shake until the sugar is dissolved.
2. Melt the butter in a large skillet over medium heat. While the butter is melting, crush the ramen noodles while still inside the package.
3. Remove the seasoning packet and throw away.
4. Add the noodles, almonds, and sesame seeds to the melted butter in the skillet.
5. Sauté while stirring frequently, until the noodle mixture is golden brown.
6. Shred the cabbage and combine the cabbage and onions in a large mixing bowl. Add the noodle mixture.
7. Pour the dressing over the salad and toss well to combine.
8. Serve immediately.

5.7 Pork Chimichurri Salad

Cooking Time: 15 minutes

Serving Size: 2

Ingredients:

- Pork chops, one pound
- Greens, six ounces
- Cherry tomatoes, two cups
- Olive oil, one tbsp.
- Vinegar, one tbsp.
- Parsley, as required
- Chipotle, half
- Oregano leaves, as required
- Salt and pepper, as required
- Chimichurri dressing, per taste

Instructions:

1. In a food processor, combine olive oil, vinegar, parsley, oregano leaves, and chipotle. Season with salt and pepper and set aside.

2. Preheat a broiler. Line a rimmed baking sheet with foil and spray with cooking oil.

3. Place pork on the baking sheet and sprinkle both sides with salt and pepper. Broil until internal temperature reaches 145 degrees, five minutes per side. Remove pork from broiler and let it rest for five minutes.

4. Meanwhile, in a large bowl, combine greens, cherry tomatoes, cheese, and chimichurri dressing to taste. Arrange salad on plates or a platter.

5. Arrange on top of salad, drizzle with additional dressing, and serve.

5.8 Spring Green Salad

Cooking Time: 30 minutes

Serving Size: 4

Ingredients:

- Salad potatoes, half pound
- Petits pois, half cup
- Asparagus, half cup
- Olive oil, four tbsp.
- Pumpkin seeds, one tbsp.
- Spring onions, four
- Baby courgettes, one cup
- Whole grain mustard, as required
- Salt and pepper, as required
- Honey, per taste
- Lemon juice, as required

Instructions:

1. To make the dressing, put all the ingredients in a small food processor or blender and process until smooth and emulsified. Season well.

2. Cook the potatoes in lightly salted boiling water for ten minutes, or until just tender, adding the petits pois for the last two minutes.

3. Drain and place in a wide, shallow serving bowl.

4. Heat a large griddle pan or heavy-based frying pan until hot. Add a tablespoon of olive oil and add the asparagus in a single layer.

5. Cook for five minutes, or until lightly charred. Remove from the pan and add to the potato mixture.

6. Wipe out the pan and add the remaining olive oil. When hot, add the courgettes, sliced side down, and cook for five minutes, or until lightly charred. Add to the potato mixture with the lettuce and spring onions.

7. Stir the dressing then pour over the salad and mix well. Scatter over the pumpkin seeds and serve.

5.9 Japanese Corn Salad

Cooking Time: 30 minutes

Serving Size: 4

Ingredients:

- Mayonnaise, one tbsp.
- Cabbage, one
- Corn, half cup
- Sugar, one tbsp.
- Salt and pepper, as per taste
- Ground sesame seeds, two tbsp.

Instructions:

1. Shred the cabbage and drain the excess water. To allow a nice texture, do not shred it too thinly.
2. To prepare the dressing, mix the ingredients together.
3. In another bowl, mix the cabbage and corn. Add the dressing and you are done.
4. Add the dressing right before serving as the cabbage tends to get watery.
5. Your dish is ready to be served.

Chapter 6: Japanese Soup Recipes

The Japanese cuisine contains a variety of healthy and nutritious soups that are loved by many people all over the world. Following are the yummy and easy to make soup recipes that you can try on your own.

6.1 Miso soup

Cooking Time: 15 minutes

Serving Size: 4

Ingredients:

- Water, four cups
- Miso paste, three tbsp.
- Green onions, two
- Dashi granules, two tbsp.
- Tofu, one block

Instructions:

1. In a medium saucepan over medium-high heat, combine dashi granules and water; bring to a boil.
2. Reduce heat to medium, and whisk in the miso paste, and then stir in tofu.
3. Separate the layers of the green onions, and add them to the soup.
4. Simmer gently for a few minutes before serving.
5. Your soup is ready to be served.

6.2 Ochazuke

Cooking Time: 5 minutes

Serving Size: 1

Ingredients:

- Dashi, one tbsp.
- Soy sauce, one tsp.
- Japanese green tea leaves, one
- Water, one cup
- Salt and pepper to taste
- Mirin, one tsp.

Instructions:

1. Combine all the ingredients in a small saucepan and bring it to a boil.
2. Pour the soup into a small teapot.
3. Put tea leaves in the pot.
4. Bring the water to the appropriate temperature for your tea and pour it into the pot.
5. Set aside for two minutes.
6. Your soup is ready to be served.

6.3 Ozoni

Cooking Time: 20 minutes

Serving Size: 4

Ingredients:

- Dashi, one cup

- Soy sauce, one tbsp.
- Sake, one tbsp.
- Chicken strips, one pound
- Water, two cups
- Salt and pepper to taste

Instructions:

1. Mix all the ingredients together and let it simmer.
2. Your soup is ready to be served.

6.4 Japanese Clear Onions Soup

Cooking Time: one hour

Serving Size: 5

Ingredients:

- Vegetable oil, two tbsp.
- Onion, one
- Carrot, one cup
- Garlic and ginger paste, one tbsp.
- Chicken broth, one cup
- Beef broth, one cup
- Salt and pepper as required

Instructions:

1. Place a large stock pot over medium-high heat.
2. Add the oil and place the onion, garlic, carrots, and ginger in the pot.
3. Sear the veggies on all sides to caramelize, making sure not to burn the garlic.

4. Pour in the chicken broth, beef broth, and water.

5. Bring to a boil.

6. Lower the heat to a low boil and simmer for at least one hour.

7. Use a skimmer to remove the vegetables from the broth.

8. Taste, then adjust salt as needed.

9. Your dish is ready to be served.

6.5 Wonton Dumplings Soup

Preparation time: 12 minutes

Cooking Time: 30 minutes

Serving Size: 6

Ingredients:

- Wonton wrappers, twenty-four
- Finely chopped scallion, one tsp.
- Finely chopped ginger, one tsp.
- Soy sauce, one tbsp.
- Brown sugar, one tsp.
- Chicken breast, shredded, two
- Fresh spinach, one cup
- Shrimp, one pound
- Water chestnuts, eight ounces
- Mushroom, sliced, one cup
- Rice wine, one tbsp.
- Ground pork, eight ounces

Instructions:

1. Bring chicken stock to a rolling boil, and then add all the ingredients.

2. Cook until chicken and shrimps are cooked through, for about 10 minutes.

3. In a bowl, mix the pork, ground shrimp, brown sugar, rice wine or sherry, soy sauce, scallions and chopped ginger.

4. Blend well and set aside for 25-30 minutes for flavors to blend.

5. Add one tsp. of the filling in the center of each wonton wrapper.

6. Wet the edges of each wonton with a little water and press them together with your fingers to seal.

7. To cook, add wontons to the boiling chicken stock and cook for 4-5 minutes.

8. Transfer to individual soup bowls and serve.

6.6 Kimchi and Tofu Soup

Cooking Time: 20 minutes

Serving Size: 2

Ingredients:

- Vegetable oil, one tbsp.
- Scallions, six
- Kimchi, half cup
- Chicken broth, one cup
- Soy sauce, three tbsp.
- Salt and pepper, as per taste

- Garlic and ginger paste, one tbsp.
- Tofu, one block
- Daikon, one

Instructions:

1. Heat oil in a large saucepan over high.
2. Cook white and pale-green parts of scallions, garlic, and ginger, stirring often, until softened and fragrant, about three minutes.
3. Add broth, then whisk in the soy sauce.
4. Add daikon and gently simmer until daikon is tender, fifteen minutes.
5. Add kimchi and tofu.
6. Simmer until tofu is heated through.
7. Carefully divide among bowls.
8. Your soup is ready to be served.

6.7 Shio Koji Mushroom Soup

Cooking Time: 20 minutes

Serving Size: 2

Ingredients:

- Soup stock, two cups
- Different mushrooms, two cups
- Salt and pepper to taste
- Shio koji, two tbsp.

Instructions:

1. Slice the mushrooms into thin slices or pieces and boil in plenty of water for about two mins.

2. Drain and add the shio koji seasoning to the hot mushrooms.

3. Wait about fifteen minutes for the flavours to develop.

4. In another saucepan, bring soup stock to the boil.

5. Add the mushrooms and salt and allow everything to heat through.

6. Spoon into bowls and serve with some nice crusty bread.

6.8 Yudofu

Cooking Time: 15 minutes

Serving Size: 2

Ingredients:

- Tofu, one block
- Mitsuba, as required
- Sake, one tbsp.
- Mirin, one tsp.
- Vegetable stock, three cups
- Water, one cup

Instructions:

1. Mix all the ingredients well and let it simmer for fifteen minutes.

2. Your soup is ready to be served.

6.9 Ojiya Rice Soup

Cooking Time: 20 minutes

Serving Size: 2

Ingredients:

- Japanese rice, one cup
- Vegetable stock, two cups
- Mixed vegetable, one cup
- Soy sauce, one tsp.
- Mirin, half tsp.
- Salt and pepper, to taste
- Water, two cups

Instructions:

1. Mix all the ingredients well and let it simmer for fifteen minutes.

2. Your soup is ready to be served.

6.10 Oshiruko Sweet Red Bean Soup

Cooking Time: 20 minutes

Serving Size: 3

Ingredients:

- Azuki sweet red beans, one cup
- Mochi rice cakes, four
- Vegetable stock, four cups

Instructions:

1. Start by adding the azuki and one cup for water to a large pan and bring it to the boil. You can adjust the amount of water depending if you prefer a thick or thin soup.

2. You can cook the mochi in a variety of ways, but grilling them gives great results so place the mochi under a hot grill for five to ten minutes.

3. Once the mochi begin expanding in the grill, they are ready and can be put into serving bowls.

4. After the azuki and water mix is boiled, take it off the heat and pour over the mochi in the serving bowls and enjoy.

6.11 Bean Paste Soup

Cooking Time: 15 minutes

Serving Size: 2

Ingredients:

- Bean paste, five tbsp.
- Vegetable soup, two cups
- Soy sauce, one tsp.
- Mirin, one tsp.
- Salt and pepper to taste

Instructions:

1. Mix all the ingredients well and let it simmer for fifteen minutes.

2. Your soup is ready to be served.

6.12 Egg Drop Soup

Cooking Time: 30 minutes

Serving Size: 6

Ingredients:

- Cornstarch, two tbsp.
- Eggs, two
- Green Onions, chopped, three
- Ginger, grated, half tsp.
- Water, two tbsp.
- Chicken broth, four cups
- Soy Sauce, one tbsp.

Instructions:

1. Mix all the ingredients together, and boil it for about thirty minutes.

2. Add the cornstarch in the end, and mix properly.

3. Your soup is ready to be served.

Chapter 7: Japanese Snacks

Japanese snacks are appreciated worldwide for the variety of snacks. The tastes are unique and also healthy. Following are some amazing snack recipes that you can try at home.

7.1 Japanese Summer Sandwiches

Cooking Time: 5 minutes

Serving Size: 2

Ingredients:

- Bread slices, six
- Strawberry, one cup
- Whipped cream, one cup

Instructions:

1. First you should prepare your bread.
2. Either whip half cup of whipping cream in a bowl until stiff and spread evenly on the bread.
3. Next, wash, cut off the stems and chop each strawberry in half down the middle.
4. Your sandwich is ready to be served.

7.2 Fresh Spring Rolls with Japanese Style Sauce

Cooking Time: 20 minutes

Serving Size: 4

Ingredients:

- Prawns, half pound
- Green beans, one cup
- Mint or coriander leaves, as required
- Rice paper wrapper, twelve
- Spring onion, half cup
- Mayonnaise, two tbsp.
- Bean chili paste, one tsp.
- Miso paste, one tsp.

Instructions:

1. Fill a small saucepan with some water and add a little salt.
2. Add the prawns and boil until they are bright pink for about five mins.
3. In a separate saucepan, boil the green beans for five mins.
4. Lay the rice paper on clean cloth.
5. Arrange the mint or coriander leaves on the bottom of the rice paper and add the prawn halves in the middle.
6. Top with the green beans and one whole chives or spring onion.
7. Sprinkle a little salt on top to taste.
8. Fold the sides in and tightly roll to ensure all ingredients are inside.
9. Make the dipping sauce by mixing all the ingredients together.
10. Serve spring rolls with the dipping sauce as a snack or side.

Cooking Time: 30 minutes

Serving Size: 6

Ingredients:

- Soy sauce, three tbsp.
- Boneless Chicken thighs, one pound
- Sake, one tbsp.
- Gaelic and ginger paste, one tsp.
- Katakuriko potato starch, a quarter cup
- Japanese mayonnaise, as required
- Cooking oil, as required

Instructions:

1. Cut chicken into bite-size pieces.
2. Add the ginger, garlic, soy sauce and cooking sake to a bowl and mix until combined.
3. Add the chicken, coat well, and allow marinating for twenty minutes.
4. Drain any excess liquid from the chicken and add your katakuriko potato starch. Mix until the pieces are fully coated.
5. Heat some cooking oil in a pan to around 180 degrees and test the temperature by dropping in some flour.
6. Fry a few pieces at a time for a few minutes until they are deep golden-brown colour, then remove and allow to drain on a wire rack or kitchen roll.
7. Serve hot or cold with some lemon wedges and a squeeze of Japanese mayonnaise.

7.4 Tazukuri Candied Sardines

Cooking Time: 15 minutes

Serving Size: 4

Ingredients:

- Toasted sesame seeds, one tbsp.
- Honey, one tbsp.
- Soy sauce, one tbsp.
- Sugar, one tbsp.
- Honey, one tbsp.
- Flavored oi, one tbsp.
- Sake, one tsp.
- Baby sardines, one cup

Instructions:

1. Gather all the ingredients. You will also need a baking sheet lined with parchment paper.
2. Put dried baby sardines in a frying pan, and toast them on medium-low heat for a few minutes or until crispy.
3. Add the sesame seeds in the frying pan and toast for two minutes.
4. Make sure to shake the pan constantly so the sesame seeds do not burn.
5. In the same frying pan, add sake, soy sauce, and sugar.
6. Add honey and oil.

7. Bring to a simmer on medium-low heat and reduce the sauce until the sauce gets thicken and you can draw a line on the surface of the pan with a silicone spatula.

8. Add the sardines back to the pan and coat with the sauce.

9. Once the sardines are coated with the sauce nicely, transfer back to the parchment paper.

10.   Your dish is ready to be served.

Cooking Time: 4 hours

Serving Size: 8

Ingredients:

- Water, five cups
- Sugar, two tbsp.
- Soy sauce, one tbsp.
- Edible gold leaf flakes, as required
- Black soybeans, one cup
- Kosher salt, as required

Instructions:

1. Gather all the ingredients.
2. Rinse black soybeans under running water and discard bad ones.
3. Put black soybeans and water in a large pot and let it soak overnight.
4. After being soaked, add sugar and salt and gently mix.
5. Start cooking over medium heat. Once boiling, you start to see white bubbles. When it is done, put an Otoshibuta and a regular pot lid.
6. The otoshibuta is to keep the soybeans under the cooking liquid.
7. Reduce heat to low and simmer for four hours or until the beans are tender.
8. Check inside the pot a few times to make sure there is enough cooking liquid.
9. Check if the beans are tender by mashing a bean with two fingers.

10. When the means are tender, add soy sauce and mix well.

11. Remove from the heat and place the parchment paper on top of the surface to prevent the beans from getting wrinkles.

12. Once cooled, keep in the refrigerator overnight so the soybeans will turn darker and absorb more flavour.

13. Your dish is ready to be served.

7.6 Takoyaki Octopus Balls

Cooking Time: 30 minutes

Serving Size: 6

Ingredients:

- Dashi stock powder, one tbsp.
- Eggs, two
- Flour, half cup
- Chopped boiled octopus, half cup
- Chopped spring onion, half cup
- Water, as required
- Tempura flakes, half tsp.
- Red picked ginger, half tsp.

Instructions:

1. Grab a large bowl and mix together eggs, flour, water and a little dashi stock.

2. Place your takoyaki plate on the gas stove on medium heat and heat up a small amount of oil in each hole.

3. Cut up your octopus into small pieces.

4. Place a piece of octopus in each of the semi-circular holes, and then fill up each hole to the top with the batter mix.

5. Now you can add the chopped spring onion, red pickled ginger and tempura flakes to each hole.

6. Once the takoyaki are about half cooked, you will need to flip them over.

7. Usually, you can only flip each takoyaki about three quarters of the way round so allow it to cook a little more before flipping it again.

8. Place a few takoyaki on a plate and smother them with loads of takoyaki sauce and Japanese mayonnaise.

9. Your dish is ready to be served.

7.7 Yakitori Grilled Skewers

Cooking Time: 10 minutes

Serving Size: 12

Ingredients:
- Teriyaki sauce, half cup
- Green shallots, two
- Chicken thigh, two pounds

Instructions:
1. Heat teriyaki sauce in a small saucepan medium-high heat. Bring to simmer and reduce to thicken the sauce.

2. Cut the white end part of the shallots into long pieces.

3. Prepare the skewers.

4. Preheat the BBQ grill and coat with olive oil.

5. Place the yakitori chicken skewers on the grill side to cook the chicken till browned.

6. Turn the skewers over and cook till other side browned or chicken meat change whitish colour.

7. Brush the Teriyaki sauce over the chicken skewers. When one side is coated, turn the skewers over and Brush Yakitori sauce over the side.

8. Repeat the above process one more time then turn the heat off.

9. Serve the yakitori skewers on rice or serve with green salad.

7.8 Sweet Ginger Meatballs

Cooking Time: 30 minutes

Serving Size: 4

Ingredients:

- Ginger and garlic paste, one tbsp.
- Eggs, one
- Ground turkey, one pound
- Sesame oil, half tsp.
- Soy sauce, four tbsp.
- Bread crumbs, half cup
- Hoisin, two tbsp.
- Diced scallions, as required
- Sesame seeds, as required

Instructions:

1. Pre-heat oven to 400 degrees and lightly grease a large baking sheet.
2. In a large bowl, add turkey, garlic, ginger, and mix well.
3. Then add egg, panko, sesame oil, and soy sauce, and mix well.
4. Roll out the meatballs and place on baking sheet.
5. Bake for ten mins and then rotate pan and bake for another ten minutes.
6. Heat a large sauté pan to medium.
7. Transfer meatballs to a large sauté pan that will fit them all.
8. In a small bowl mix the remaining soy sauce and hoisin.

9. Coat and turn meatballs in sauce as it bubbles and thickens and let cook for a couple of minutes.

10. Remove meatballs, add to a bowl and pour remaining sauce on meatballs.

11. Serve as an appetizer or over a layer of rice.

7.9 Satsuma Age Fried Fish Cake with Vegetables

Cooking Time: 30 minutes

Serving Size: 4

Ingredients:

- Sugar, two tbsp.
- Eggs, one
- Fish fillet, one pound
- Salt, as required
- Ginger juice, half tsp.
- Water, two tbsp.
- Mix vegetables, two cups
- Soy Sauce, one tbsp.

Instructions:

1. Cut fish fillet into small pieces so that it is easier to make paste in a food processor.

2. Add fish pieces, sake, ginger juice, salt and sugar to a food processor and whizz until the mixture becomes paste.

3. Add egg to the fish paste and blend well.

4. Add all the vegetable mixture in a large bowl and mix well ensuring that vegetable pieces are evenly coated with corn flour.

5. This will allow the vegetables to stick to the paste better.

6. Add the fish paste to the bowl and mix well.

7. Heat oil in a deep-frying pan or a skillet to 170 degrees.

8. Take the fish cake mixture and make a ball.

9. Fry until bottom side of the fish cake is golden brown.

10. Turn it over to cook until golden brown.

11. Remove the fish cake and drain oil on a rack or kitchen paper.

12. Serve while hot or at room temperature with lemon wedges, or grated ginger.

7.10 Sweet and Salty Nori Seaweed Popcorn

Cooking Time: 30 minutes

Serving Size: 6

Ingredients:

- Black sesame seeds, one tbsp.
- Brown sugar, one tbsp.
- Salt, half tsp.
- Coconut oil, half tsp.
- Popcorn kernel, half cup
- Butter, two tbsp.
- Nori seaweed flakes, one tbsp.

Instructions:

1. In a pestle and mortar, grind the nori seaweed flakes, sesame seeds, sugar and salt to a fine powder.

2. Melt the coconut oil in a large, heavy-bottomed saucepan.

3. Add popcorn kernels, cover with a lid and cook over a medium heat until they pop.

4. Immediately add the rest of the corn after the corn is popped, replace the lid and cook, shaking the pan occasionally until all the kernels are popped.

5. Transfer the popped corn to a large bowl and pour over the melted butter, if using.

6. Sprinkle over your sweet and salty nori mixture and use your hands to mix well until every piece is coated.

7. Top with the remaining sesame seeds.

Chapter 8: Japanese Desserts

Japanese cuisine is famous for its amazing dessert ranges. Here in this section where we will discuss the yummiest dessert recipes of Japan.

8.1 Kinako Dango

Cooking Time: 5 minutes

Serving Size: 4

Ingredients:

- Kinako, half cup
- Granulated sugar, two tbsp.
- Cold water, half cup
- Dango powder, one cup
- Kosher salt, half tsp.

Instructions:

1. In a mixing bowl add Dango powder and water. Mix well until well combined.
2. Grab a little dough and shape into a ball.
3. Lay it on a plate and repeat until all the dough is used.
4. Set aside a bowl of cold water.
5. Add dango balls to boiling water and boil until they rise to the top.
6. Drain and add to cold water. Leave for a few minutes until they cool down and drain.
7. In another mixing bowl, add kinako, sugar and salt, and mix well.

8. Put a half of the kinako mixture in a serving bowl, add dango balls, and top with leftover kinako.

9. Your meal is ready to be served.

8.2 Japanese Style Pumpkin Pudding

Cooking Time: 25 minutes

Serving Size: 2

Ingredients:

- Pumpkin puree, one cup
- Sugar, three tbsp.
- Vanilla extract, one tsp.
- Eggs, two
- Gelatin powder, two tbsp.
- Maple syrup, as required

Instructions:

1. Dissolve the gelatin powder with the milk.

2. Meanwhile, put the pumpkin puree and sugar in a bowl, stir, and microwave on high for thirty seconds.

3. Stir in the milk and gelatin mix and add it to the pumpkin and sugar. Stir in the eggs and vanilla extract and combine well.

4. Get rid of the unblended bits left in the strainer.

5. Place a deep pan or pot over a burner and put the ramekins inside.

6. Turn the heat on and bring the water to a boil.

7. Turn the heat off and check the firmness of the puddings. The texture should be a little firm but still creamy like pudding.

8. Cool the puddings in the fridge until they are completely chilled.

9. Pour two tablespoons of pure maple syrup on top of each pudding before serving.

8.3 Dorayaki

Cooking Time: 15 minutes

Serving Size: 6

Ingredients:

- Honey, two tbsp.
- Eggs, two
- Sugar, one cup
- Flour, one cup
- Baking powder, one tsp.
- Red bean paste, half cup

Instructions:

1. Gather all the ingredients.

2. In a large bowl, combine eggs, sugar, and honey and whisk well until the mixture becomes fluffy.

3. Sift flour and baking powder into the bowl and mix all together.

4. The batter should be slightly smoother now.

5. Heat a large non-stick frying pan over medium-low heat. It is best to take your time and heat slowly.

6. When you see the surface of the batter starting to bubble, flip over and cook the other side.

7. Put the red bean paste in the centre.

8. Wrap dorayaki with plastic wrap until ready to be served.

8.4 Fluffy Japanese Cheesecake

Cooking Time: 50 minutes

Serving Size: 4-5

Ingredients:

- Vanilla ice cream
- Brownie mix, one box
- Hot fudge sauce

Instructions:

1. Preheat oven to 350 degrees.

2. Cut strips of foil to line jumbo muffin tin cups.

3. Layer strips in crisscross manner to use as lifting handles when brownies are done.

4. Spray foil in a pan with cooking spray.

5. Prepare brownie batter as described on the back of the box or according to your favorite recipe.

6. Divide batter evenly among muffin tin cups. Muffin cups will be about 3/4 full.

7. Place muffin tin on the rimmed baking sheet and bake in preheated oven for 40-50 minutes.

8. Remove from oven and cool in the pan for 5 minutes, then transfer to a cooling rack for ten additional minutes.

9. You may need to use a butter knife or icing spatula to loosen the sides of each brownie and

then lift out of the muffin pan using the foil handles.

10. Serve warm brownie on a plate topped with a scoop of vanilla ice cream and hot fudge sauce.

8.5 Matcha Ice cream

Cooking Time: 5 minutes

Serving Size: 2

Ingredients:

- Matcha powder, three tbsp.
- Half and half, two cups
- Kosher salt, a pinch
- Sugar, half cup

Instructions:

1. In a medium saucepan, whisk together the half and half, sugar, and salt.
2. Start cooking the mixture over medium heat, and add green tea powder.
3. Remove from the heat and transfer the mixture to a bowl sitting in an ice bath. When the mixture is cool, cover with plastic wrap and chill in the refrigerator.
4. Your dish is ready to be served.

8.6 Taiyaki

Cooking Time: 15 minutes

Serving Size: 5

Ingredients:

- Cake flour, two cups
- Baking powder, one tsp.
- Baking soda, half tsp.
- Sugar, one cup
- Egg, two
- Milk, half cup

Instructions:

1. Sift the cake flour, baking powder and baking soda into a large bowl.
2. Add the sugar and whisk well to combine.
3. In a medium bowl, whisk the egg and then add the milk.
4. Combine the dry ingredients with wet ingredients and whisk well.
5. Pour the batter into a measuring cup or jug.
6. Heat the Taiyaki pan and grease the pan with vegetable oil using a brush.
7. Fill the Taiyaki pan mould about 60% full over medium-low heat.
8. Close the lid and immediately turn.
9. Then flip and cook. Open and check to see if Taiyaki is golden coloured.
10. Let Taiyaki cool on a wire rack.
11. Your dish is ready to be served.

8.7 Zenzai

Cooking Time: 15 minutes

Serving Size: 4

Ingredients:

- Mochi, one cup
- Red beans, one cup
- Sugar, three tbsp.

Instructions:

1. Place red beans, and five cups of water in a pot.
2. Bring to a boil and cook for five minutes, and then, strain the beans and discard the water they were cooked in.
3. Now, drain the beans, reserving the water they were cooked in.
4. Put drained beans into the pot, add sugar, and cook over medium heat for ten minutes, stirring constantly.
5. Then, pour in the water from cooking the beans, season with sugar, and stir over low heat.
6. Bake mochi over a grill or in a toaster oven until they expand and brown slightly.
7. Put mochi into a serving bowl and cover with a scoop of bean soup.
8. Your dish is ready to be served.

8.8 Okoshi

Cooking Time: 10 minutes

Serving Size: 3

Ingredients:

- Cooked rice, one cup
- Tempura oil, one tbsp.
- Sugar, one cup
- Puffed rice, one cup
- Peanuts, half cup

Instructions:

1. Spread the cooked rice on a baking sheet in a thin layer and place it on a flat sieve or a serving tray.

2. When the rice becomes translucent and crispy, it is ready for further preparation. First, break down any lumps using your fingers.

3. Line a mould for okoshi with baking paper.

4. Heat tempura oil to 180 degrees and deep fry the rice.

5. Mix sugar with water and cook over medium heat until the syrup starts simmering, then lower the heat and, if you wish, add peanuts.

6. Combine fried, puffed rice and sugar syrup quickly, and transfer to a container. Cover the top with a baking sheet, and press with a heavy and flat object.

7. Cut into small pieces and serve.

8.9 Dango

Cooking Time: 10 minutes

Serving Size: 6

Ingredients:

- Joshinko rice flour, one cup
- Shiratamako rice flour, one cup
- Sugar, half cup
- Hot water, as required

Instructions:

1. Mix together the joshinko non-glutinous rice flour, shiratamako glutinous rice flour and sugar.

2. Add the hot water little by little, mixing well.

3. Cover the bowl you mixed your dango mixture in and microwave for a few minutes. Dampen your hands again and roll the dough into evenly sized balls.

4. Your dish is ready to be served.

8.10 Kasutera

Cooking Time: 50 minutes

Serving Size: 24

Ingredients:

- Milk, one cup
- Honey, two tbsp.
- Flour, two cups
- Sugar, one cup

Instructions:

1. Set the oven to preheat to 170 degrees.

2. First, coat the bottom and the sides of a baking pan with butter or shortening, and then line it with baking paper, so that a portion of the paper is hanging over the sides of the pan.

3. Sprinkle the bottom of the pan with sugar.

4. Bring a pot of water to a boil, and then remove from the heat.

5. Whisk milk and honey together and double sift the flour.

6. Add the eggs and the sugar to the bowl.

7. Next, whisk in the milk and honey mixture, and then add flour tablespoon by tablespoon, whisking all the time until incorporated.

8. When the cake is cool enough to handle, put the cake into a plastic bag and seal. Refrigerate for a few hours.

9. Your dish is ready to be served.

8.11 Daifuku

Cooking Time: 10 minutes

Serving Size: 6

Ingredients:

- Swedish dried peas, two tbsp.
- Caster sugar, two tbsp.
- Rice flour, two cups
- Potato starch, one cup
- Anko red bean paste, two tbsp.

Instructions:

1. Place the Swedish red peas in a small saucepan and pour enough water to cover the red peas.
2. Bring it to simmer over low heat and cook for ten minutes.
3. Divide the anko sweet red bean paste into six balls.
4. Place the Shiratamako in a mixing bowl and add sugar and water.
5. Cover your hand with katakuriko potato starch and spread the mochi dough out with your hand.
6. Place the Swedish red peas over the mochi dough and fold the mochi dough in half.
7. Take one piece of dough on your palm and flat it.
8. Close the mochi ends at the top with your well dusted finger and shape it into a nice round shaped daifuku mochi.

Chapter 9: Ramen and Sushi Recipes

Japanese ramen and sushi are famous worldwide. They are appreciated by many individuals all around the globe. Following are some recipes you can make at home:

9.1 Shoyu Ramen

Cooking Time: 30 minutes

Serving Size: 4

Ingredients:

- Chashu, one cup
- Nitamago, as required
- Shiitake, as required
- La-yu, as required
- Nori, half cup
- Ramen, four packs
- Dashi, half cup

Instructions:

1. In a pot of salted boiling water, cook ramen, stirring with tongs or chopsticks until cooked, about one minute.

2. In a small saucepan over medium heat, warm dashi and shiitake until barely simmering.

3. Cook for one minute and remove from heat.

4. Set shiitake aside.

5. Add dashi and noodles to serving bowl.

6. Top with chashu, nitamago, shiitake, green onion, a drizzle of la-yu, and nori, if desired.

9.2 Miso Ramen

Cooking Time: 10 minutes

Serving Size: 2

Ingredients:

- Miso paste, two tbsp.
- Mix vegetables, one cup
- Ramen, two packs
- Soy sauce, one tbsp.

Instructions:

1. Cook the ramen, and boil the vegetables.
2. Now mix all the remaining ingredients, and serve hot.

9.3 Simple Homemade Chicken Ramen

Cooking Time: 10 minutes

Serving Size: 2

Ingredients:

- Chicken, one cup
- Ramen noodles, two packs
- Oil, one tsp.
- Salt and pepper to taste

Instructions:

1. Cook the ramen, and chicken.
2. Now mix all the other ingredients, and serve hot.

9.4 Vegetarian Ramen

Cooking Time: 10 minutes

Serving Size: 2

Ingredients:

- Mix vegetables, one cup
- Ramen noodles, two packs
- Oil, one tsp.
- Salt and pepper to taste

Instructions:

1. Cook the ramen, and vegetables.
2. Now mix all the other ingredients, and serve hot.

9.5 Ramen Noodles

Cooking Time: 10 minutes

Serving Size: 2

Ingredients:

- Ramen noodles, two packs
- Miso paste, two tbsp.
- Soy Sauce, one tbsp.

Instructions:

1. Mix all the ingredients together, and cook well for ten minutes.
2. Your dish is ready to be served

9.6 Pork Ramen

Cooking Time: 10 minutes

Serving Size: 2

Ingredients:

- Pork meat, one cup
- Ramen noodles, two packs
- Oil, one tsp.
- Salt and pepper to taste

Instructions:

1. Cook the ramen, and pork meat.
2. Now mix all the ingredients, and serve hot.

9.7 Instant Ramen

Cooking Time: 10 minutes

Serving Size: 2

Ingredients:

- Instant ramen noodles, two packs
- Instant spice mix, two tbsp.
- Water, three cups

Instructions:

1. Mix all the ingredients together and cook for ten minutes.
2. Your dish is ready to be served.

9.8 Sushi

Cooking Time: 5 minutes

Serving Size: 4

Ingredients:

- Sesame oil, half tsp.
- Green onions/scallions, two
- Toasted white sesame seeds, two tbsp.
- Spicy Mayo, two tbsp.
- Sushi rice (cooked and seasoned), one and a half cup
- Sashimi-grade tuna, four ounces
- Sriracha sauce, three tsp.

Instructions:

1. In a medium bowl, combine the tuna, Sriracha sauce, sesame oil, and some of the green onion.

2. Lay a sheet of nori, shiny side down, on the bamboo mat. Wet your fingers in water and spread ¾ cup of the rice evenly onto nori sheet.

3. Sprinkle the rice with sesame seeds.

4. Turn the sheet of nori over so that the rice side is facing down.

5. Line the edge of nori sheet at the bottom end of the bamboo mat.

6. Place half of the tuna mixture at the bottom end of the nori sheet.

7. Grab the bottom edge of the bamboo mat while keeping the fillings in place with your fingers, roll into a tight cylinder form.

8. With a very sharp knife, cut the roll in half and then cut each half into three pieces.

9. Put a dollop of spicy mayo on top of each sushi and garnish with the remaining green onion.

10. Your dish is ready to be served.

9.9 Japanese Sushi Rolls

Cooking Time: 60 minutes

Serving Size: 4

Ingredients:

- Lemon, half
- Nori sheets, two
- Sushi rice, two cups
- Shrimp tempura, eight pieces
- Tobiko, two tbsp.
- Unagi (eel)
- Persian/Japanese cucumbers, one
- Avocados, one

Instructions:

1. Gather all the ingredients.
2. Cut cucumber lengthwise into quarters.
3. Remove the seeds, and then cut in half lengthwise.
4. Cut the avocado in half lengthwise around the seed, and twist the two halves until they are separate.
5. Hack the knife edge into the pit. Hold the skin of the avocado with the other hand, and twist in counter directions.
6. Remove the skin, and slice the avocado widthwise.
7. Gently press the avocado slices with your fingers, and then keep pressing gently, and evenly with the side of the knife until the length of avocado is about the length of sushi roll.

8. Wrap the bamboo mat with plastic wrap, and place half of the nori sheet, shiny side down.

9. Turn it over and put the shrimp tempura, cucumber strips, and tobiko at the bottom end of the nori sheet.

10. If you like to put unagi, place it inside here as well.

11. From the bottom end, start rolling nori sheet over the filling tightly, and firmly with bamboo mat until the bottom end reaches the nori sheet.

12. Place the bamboo mat over the roll and tightly squeeze the roll.

13. Using the side of the knife, place the avocado on top of the roll.

14. Place plastic wrap over the roll and then put the bamboo mat over.

15. Cut the roll into 8 pieces with the knife.

16. Put tobiko on each piece of sushi, and drizzle spicy mayo, and sprinkle black sesame seeds on top.

17. Your dish is ready to be served.

Chapter 10: Most Popular and Alternative Japanese Recipes

Japanese cuisine remains rooted in its traditions, while embracing a certain amount of fusion from other cultures. Following are some traditional and alternative recipes:

10.1 Sashimi

Cooking Time: 20-30 seconds

Serving Size: 3

Ingredients:

- Tuna, one pound
- Salmon, one pound, sesame oil, two tbsp.
- Coriander leaves, as required

Instructions:

1. Drizzle the tuna and salmon with sesame seed oil, turning it over to ensure even coverage on all sides.

2. Sprinkle a generous helping of dried and chopped coriander leaves over the tuna, and salmon filet.

3. Cook the fish for only fifteen to twenty seconds.

4. Your dish is ready to be served with your preferred sauce.

10.2 Unadon

Cooking Time: 20-30 seconds

Ingredients:

- Sesame oil, two tbsp.
- Unagi eel, two pounds
- Japanese pepper one tbsp.
- Coriander leaves, one tbsp.

Instructions:

1. Drizzle the unagi with sesame seed oil, turning it over to ensure even coverage on all sides.

2. Sprinkle a generous amount of Japanese pepper, and chopped coriander leaves over the unagi.

3. Cook the fish for only fifteen to twenty seconds.

4. Your dish is ready to be served.

10.3 Tempura

Cooking Time: 10 minutes

Serving: 2

Ingredients:

- Plain flour, four tbsp.
- Prawns, one pound
- Mix vegetables, one cup
- Mayonnaise, half tsp.
- Water, two tbsp.

Instructions:

1. Prepare the prawn and vegetables and set aside.
2. Place the flour, and add icy cold water and mayonnaise.
3. Set aside in fridge until all ingredients and oil are ready.
4. Fill a deep pan or deep-fryer with vegetable oil and heat until 180 degrees.
5. Add each ingredient to the batter individually to coat them and put them into the oil.
6. Fry each ingredient.
7. Your dish is ready to be served with your preferred sauce

10.4 Soba

Cooking Time: 10 minutes

Serving Size: 2

Ingredients:

- Japanese noodles, one pack
- Sesame seeds, as required
- Sesame oil, one tbsp.
- Green Onions, chopped, three
- Ginger, grated, half tsp.
- Soy Sauce, one tbsp.

Instructions:

1. Boil the noodles properly and then mix all the ingredients together while on heat.
2. Your dish is ready to be served.

10.5 Udon

Cooking Time: 15 minutes

Serving Size: 2

Ingredients:

- Cornstarch, two tbsp.
- Japanese noodles, one pack
- Green Onions, chopped, three
- Ginger, grated, half tsp.
- Water, two tbsp.
- Chicken broth, four cups

- Soy Sauce, one tbsp.

Instructions:

1. Mix all the ingredients together and let it cook for fifteen minutes.
2. Now add the corn flour mixed in water.
3. Cook for five minutes.
4. Your dish is ready to be served.

10.6 Sukiyaki

Cooking Time: 30 minutes

Serving Size: 6

Ingredients:

- Dried vermicelli, two cups
- Tofu slices, six
- Shiitake mushrooms, half cup
- Enoki mushrooms, half cup
- Napa cabbage, one cup
- Tong ho, half cup
- Scallions, one cup
- Vegetable oil, two tbsp.
- Beef slices, six slices

Instructions:

1. Prepare all your sukiyaki ingredients, the tofu slices, rehydrated shiitake mushrooms, enoki mushrooms, napa cabbage, tong ho, and scallions.
2. Soak the dried vermicelli noodles in water for ten minutes.

3. Heat a tablespoon vegetable oil in the pan.

4. Fry the white parts of the scallions in the oil for two minutes.

5. In the pan with the scallions, add the sliced beef.

6. Sear the beef for a few seconds, and add a drizzle of your sukiyaki sauce.

7. Add the rest of your sukiyaki sauce and two cups stock.

8. Bring to a boil, and add the tofu, mushrooms, napa cabbage, and tong ho to the pot in sections.

9. Also drain the vermicelli noodles you soaked and add them to the pot.

10.   Remove the cover, and add the beef back to the pot.

11.   Sprinkle with the chopped scallions, and enjoy with rice and egg yolk.

10.7 Oden

Cooking Time: 30 minutes

Serving Size: 6

Ingredients:

- Dashi, three cups
- Fish cakes, six
- Fish balls, six
- Eggs, six
- Konnyaku, two
- Kombu, two
- Japanese mustard, two tbsp.
- Soy sauce, two tsp.
- Mirin, two tsp.
- Sake, two tsp.
- Togarashi, as required

Instructions:

1. Rinse the fish cakes and fish balls with running water, remove the excess oil from the fish cakes and fish balls.

2. In a soup pot, bring the dashi, water, kombu strips to boil.

3. Add the daikon and stew on low heat until they are cooked through.

4. Add the hard-boiled eggs, konnyaku, and fish cakes.

5. Add the soy sauce, mirin and sake. Turn the heat to low and simmer for fifteen minutes.

6. Serve the Oden warm with Japanese mustard and Togarashi.

10.8 Gohan - Steamed Rice

Cooking Time: 10 minutes

Serving Size: 2

Ingredients:

- Japanese rice, one cup
- Water, one and a half cup
- Salt for taste

Instructions:

1. Wash the rice and then cook it properly.
2. Pour water into a pan and boil it and add rice as well as salt.
3. Cover for ten minutes.
4. Your dish is ready to be served.

Cooking Time: 15 minutes

Serving Size: 4

Ingredients:

- Pork loin, one pound
- Eggs, two
- Bread crumbs, half cup
- Cabbage, one

Instructions:

1. Slash the fat rimming one side of the loin cutlet to keep the meat from curling when deep fried.

2. Sprinkle salt and pepper both sides of each cutlet.

3. Dredge each in flour, then dip into beaten eggs and press into bread crumbs to coat both sides.

4. Heat a large skillet with about half inch of oil until hot.

5. Deep-fry until golden brown, about five minutes, turning them once or twice. Drain the cutlets on paper towels and cut the pork into bite-size strips that can be eaten with chopsticks.

6. Arrange the pork on a platter lined with the shredded cabbage, and garnish with lemon wedges.

7. Serve your preferred sauce on the side for dipping, or pour it over the pork and cabbage.

10.10 Wagashi

Cooking Time: 30 minutes

Serving Size: 3

Ingredients:

- Shiro-an, one cup
- Water, half cup
- Sugar, half cup
- Rice flour, one cup

Instructions:

1. Combine the water, sugar, and rice flour.
2. Stir this in with 600 grams of the shiroan and heat over medium heat.
3. You should end up with a tacky dough that can be shaped with your fingers.
4. Let it cool down.
5. Make into various shapes.
6. Your dish is ready to be served.

10.11 Japanese Matcha Green Tea

Cooking Time: 5 minutes

Serving Size: 1

Ingredients:

- Matcha tea leaves, one tsp.
- Water, one cup

Instructions:

1. Mix all the ingredients together and then let it boil for five minutes.

2. Drain the tea. Your tea is ready.

Chapter 11: Japanese Vegetarian Recipes

Japan is known for its variety of vegetarian cuisine, Japanese love vegetables, and tend to make more vegetarian meals. Following are some amazing vegetarian recipes:

11.1 Kenchin Vegetable Soup

Cooking Time: 30 minutes

Serving Size: 3

Ingredients:

- Dashi, one cup
- Mix vegetables, one cup
- Taro, half cup
- Abura age, one cup
- Mirin, two tbsp.
- Soy Sauce, one tbsp.
- Salt, as required
- Sesame oil, two tbsp.

Instructions:

1. Begin by peeling your daikon, burdock and carrot, and then cut them into bite sized chunks.

2. Scrub the taro well with a vegetable brush, making sure any dirt is removed.

3. In a bowl, soak the abura age in hot water to remove any excess oil, and then slice into bite sized pieces.

4. Add the dashi, vegetables and abura age fried tofu to a pan and bring to boil. Add the soy sauce, mirin, salt and sesame oil, and simmer until the vegetables are tender and soft.

5. Serve and garnish with the spring onion.

11.2 Vegan Japanese Omelette

Cooking Time: 10 minutes

Serving Size: 2

Ingredients:

- Vegan mayo, as required
- Wheat flour, one cup
- Nori, one
- Soy sauce, one tsp.
- Water, one cup
- Salt and pepper to taste
- Oil, two tbsp.

Instructions:

1. In a large mixing bowl, combine all ingredients and stir together so you have a thick dough.

2. Heat a drop of oil in a frying pan and heat on high.

3. Add a scoop of dough and flatten.

4. Reduce flame to medium heat and gently sear each side of the omelette for five minutes.

5. Serve your dish with vegan mayo.

11.3 Japanese Vegetable Pancake

Cooking Time: 25 minutes

Serving Size: 2

Ingredients:

- Dashi, half cup
- Eggs, two
- Bacon slices, three
- Okonomiyaki sauce, as required
- Mayyonaise, two tbsp.
- Cabbage, half cup
- Green onion, as required
- Flour, one tbsp.

Instructions:

1. Mix the flour, dashi, egg and cabbage in a large bowl.
2. Heat oil in large pan over medium heat, pour in mixture, flatten, top with the bacon slices and cook until golden brown on both sides, about ten minutes per side.
3. Top with okonomiyaki sauce, mayonnaise, and green onion slices.
4. Your dish is ready to be served.

11.4 Vegetarian Japanese Curry

Cooking Time: 30 minutes

Serving Size: 4

Ingredients:

- Mixed vegetables, two cups
- Green Onions, chopped, three
- Ginger, grated, half tsp.
- Tomato puree, one cup
- Vegetable broth, two cups
- Salt and pepper as required
- Soy Sauce, one tbsp.

Instructions:

1. Mix all the ingredients together, and let it simmer for thirty minutes.
2. Your meal is ready to be served.

11.5 Vegetable Tempura

Cooking Time: 10 minutes

Serving Size: 2

Ingredients:

- Plain flour, four tbsp.
- Mix vegetables, one cup
- Mayonnaise, half tsp.
- Water, two tbsp.

Instructions:

1. Place the flour, and add icy cold water and mayonnaise.
2. Set aside in fridge until all ingredients and oil are ready.
3. Fill a deep pan or deep-fryer with vegetable oil and heat until 180 degrees.
4. Add each ingredient to the batter individually to coat them and put them into the oil.
5. Fry each ingredient.
6. Your dish is ready to be served with your preferred sauce.

11.6 Japanese Edamame

Cooking Time: 10 minutes

Serving Size: 2

Ingredients:

- Edamame, one cup
- Soy Sauce, one tbsp.
- Sesame oil, one tsp.
- Salt and pepper to taste

Instructions:

1. Boil edamame for a few minutes.
2. In a pan over high heat, add sesame oil.
3. When the oil is hot, almost smoking, add edamame pods and fry for two minutes.
4. Add soy sauce and stir until the sauce is evaporated.
5. Season with salt and lots of black pepper.
6. Your dish is ready to be served.

11.7 Japanese Eggplant Curry

Cooking Time: 30 minutes

Serving Size: 4

Ingredients:

- Eggplant, two
- Green Onions, chopped, three
- Ginger, grated, half tsp.
- Tomato puree, one cup
- Vegetable broth, two cups
- Salt and pepper as required
- Soy Sauce, one tbsp.

Instructions:

1. Mix all the ingredients together, and let it simmer for thirty minutes.

2. Your meal is ready to be served.

11.8 Mushroom and Tofu Potstickers

Cooking Time: 15 minutes

Serving Size: 5

Ingredients:

- Sesame oil, two tbsp.
- Mushrooms, one cup
- Red pepper, half tsp.
- Cabbage, half cup
- Wonton wrappers, ten
- Scallions, half cup
- Ginger and garlic paste, half tsp.
- Olive oil, two tbsp.
- Tofu, one block
- Soy Sauce, one tbsp.

Instructions:

1. Heat a frying pan and add the olive oil.
2. Sauté the crumbled tofu, mushrooms, cabbage, ginger, and garlic for a few minutes.
3. When the tofu and mushrooms are almost cooked, add the scallions, soy sauce, sesame oil, and optional red pepper flakes, stirring well to combine.
4. Add the mixture to wonton wrappers and then steam them for five minutes.
5. Your dish is ready to be served with your preferred sauce.

11.9 Vegetable Teppanyaki

Cooking Time: 10 minutes

Serving Size: 2

Ingredients:

- Mixed vegetables, two cups
- Sesame oil, two tbsp.
- Salt and pepper to taste
- Cooking wine, two tbsp.
- Soy Sauce, one tbsp.

Instructions:

1. In a skillet over high heat, add two tablespoon oil.
2. Add carrots and cook until almost tender.
3. Add the rest of the vegetables and stir fry.
4. Pour in soy sauce and cooking wine.
5. Season with salt and pepper.
6. Your meal is ready to be served.

11.10 Naturally Sweet Red Bean Daifuku

Cooking Time: 10 minutes

Serving Size: 6

Ingredients:

- Sweet red beans, two tbsp.
- Caster sugar, two tbsp.
- Rice flour, two cups
- Potato starch, one cup

Instructions:

1. Place the sweet red beans in a small saucepan and pour enough water to cover the red peas.

2. Bring it to simmer over low heat and cook for ten minutes.

3. Place the red beans in a mixing bowl and add sugar and water.

4. Cover your hand with katakuriko potato starch and spread the mochi dough out with your hand.

5. Place the Swedish red peas over the mochi dough and fold the mochi dough in half.

6. Close the mochi ends at the top with your well dusted finger and shape it into a nice round shaped daifuku mochi.

7. Your dish is ready to be served.

11.11 Japanese Carrot Pickles

Cooking Time: 5 hours

Serving Size: 3-4

Ingredients:

- Rice vinegar, half cup
- Sugar, two tbsp.
- Sesame seeds, as required
- Carrots, two cups

Instructions:

1. In a large cup, whisk together the rice vinegar and sugar until it dissolves completely.

2. Pour the vinegar mixture over all of the carrots, and leave it for five hours.

3. Sprinkle sesame seeds on top and serve.

11.12 Mango Mochi

Cooking Time: 20 minutes

Serving Size: 5-6

Ingredients:

- Potato starch, two tbsp.
- Water, as required
- Rice flour, one cup
- Green Onions, chopped, three
- Mongo bites, one cup
- Whipped cream, one cup
- Sugar, two cups

- Cream stabilizer one tbsp.

Instructions:

1. In a small cup, add sugar and cream stabilizer.
2. In another bowl, add whipping cream and blend with an electric hand mixer for a few seconds. Then add the sugar mix.
3. Add the whipped cream in the moulds.
4. Place the mango bits on the cream. Then cover with the remaining whipped cream.
5. In a bowl, add glutinous rice flour, sugar and water.
6. Heat over medium heat, stir constantly, until smooth and silky.
7. Spread the potato starch onto your working surface or chopping board.
8. Pull out one filling from the freezer.
9. Pull the edges of the mochi disc over the filling so as to cover it.
10. Your dish is ready to be served.

11.13 Japanese Green Avocado Salad

Cooking Time: 10 minutes

Serving Size: 2

Ingredients:

- Cucumber, one
- Snowpeas, half cup
- Avocado, one
- Cabbage, half
- Green salad dressing, half cup
- Salt and pepper, per taste

Instructions:

1. Bring a small saucepan of water to a boil and blanch the snowpeas.
2. Peel the cucumber and slice into very thin rounds.
3. For the dressing, whisk all the ingredients together in a small bowl.
4. Combine all the green ingredients in a large bowl, pour the dressing over the top and gently toss with your hands to coat them.
5. Your dish is ready to be served.

11.14 Sweet Potatoes and Avocado Green Salad

Cooking Time: 10 minutes

Serving Size: 2

Ingredients:

- Sweet potato, one
- Avocado, one
- Green salad dressing, half cup
- Salt and pepper to taste
- Cucumber, one

Instructions:

1. Boil the sweet potato for ten minutes.
2. Cut into pieces and mix the rest of the ingredients.
3. Your dish is ready to be served.

11.15 Japanese Baked Sweet Potato

Cooking Time: 30 minutes

Serving Size: 3

Ingredients:

- Sweet potatoes, three
- Soy Sauce, one tbsp.
- Sesame oil, two tbsp.
- Salt and pepper, to taste

Instructions:

1. Cut the sweet potatoes into half and add the rest of the ingredients on it.

2. Bake it at 180 degrees for ten minutes.

3. Your dish is ready to be served.

11.16 Japanese Fried Rice

Cooking Time: 30 minutes

Serving Size: 4

Ingredients:

- Fish sauce, two tbsp.
- Egg, one
- Soy sauce, half cup
- Cooked Japanese rice, three cups
- Tomatoes, two
- Cilantro, half cup
- Salt and pepper, to taste
- Vegetable oil, two tbsp.
- Toasted walnuts, half cup
- Chicken breast, eight ounces
- Onion, one
- Scallions, half cup
- Minced garlic, one tsp.

Instructions:

1. Heat a large nonstick pan over high heat.
2. Meanwhile, season chicken lightly with salt and pepper.
3. When the pan is very hot, add two tsp of the oil.
4. When the oil is hot, add the chicken and cook on high until it is browned all over and cooked through.

5. Remove chicken from pan and set aside, add the eggs, pinch of salt and cook a minute or two until done.

6. Add the remaining oil to the pan and add the onion, scallions and garlic.

7. Sauté for a minute, add the chili pepper if using, tomatoes and stir in all the rice.

8. Add the soy sauce and fish sauce stir to mix all the ingredients.

9. Keep stirring a few minutes, and then add egg and chicken back to the wok.

10. Adjust soy sauce if needed and stir well another 30 seconds.

11. Your dish is ready to be served.

11.17 Kenchinjiru

Cooking Time: 30 minutes

Serving Size: 3

Ingredients:

- Dashi, one cup
- Mix vegetables, one cup
- Taro, half cup
- Abura age, one cup
- Mirin, two tbsp.
- Soy Sauce, one tbsp.
- Salt, as required
- Sesame oil, two tbsp.
- Japanese seven spice, two tbsp.
- Sesame oil, two tbsp.
- Sake, one tsp.
- Tofu, one block.

Instructions:

1. Mix all the ingredients together and let it simmer for thirty minutes straight.
2. Serve and garnish with the spring onion.

The recipes mentioned in this chapter are very easy to make and will fill your craving needs for delicious Japanese cuisine.

Conclusion

Japanese Cuisine is known for its variety of dishes and its vast combination of rare spices that are usually grown only in Japan. This cuisine has been out there from the 18th century but has entered the United States of America from the times when trade began between the two countries, and Japanese people started to move in to America for various purposes.

Today, Japanese cuisine is not only liked by Japanese people residing all over the world but also by other people that live in America. There are various restaurant chains and eateries that make delicious Japanese food but what is better than cooking your favorite meals all by yourself at home.

This book contains all the details that you need to know regarding Japanese cuisine. You can get to know about its history, the different spices that are used in Japanese meals and their various health benefits. So, now you have all the knowledge you need to start cooking Japanese food on your own. This book also contains more than 100 different recipes that include breakfast, lunch, dinner, soups, salads, sweets, traditional as well as vegetarian meals. So, do not wait more, start cooking from today and eat your favorite Japanese healthy and yummy meals at home.

Printed in Great Britain
by Amazon